The Cigarette Diaries

By Frank J. Pratt
With Rebecca Pratt

Published by Cave Art Press, Anacortes, WA 98221
An imprint of Douglass, Hemingway & Co., LLC
CaveArtPress.com

ISBN-13: 978-1934199-220

Editor and book designer: Arlene Cook
Cover design: Rose Unes
Manuscript readers: Réanne Hemingway-Douglass, Kathleen Kaska, Lisa Wright
Photographs by Frank Pratt, Rebecca Pratt and Arlene Cook
Maps by Ken Morrison

To The Curious!

This book contains notes of a nature meaningless, I believe, to anyone else but myself. You are perfectly welcome to read them; however, don't say I didn't warn you.

Frank J. Pratt
2nd Lieutenant
US Army Air Corps

Frank Pratt, 1944

CONTENTS

LIST OF MAPS

Foreword

Frank J. Pratt was born on October 24, 1915, in the then-thriving town of Blanchard, Washington, seventy-five miles north of Seattle. His father, Thomas, worked in the lumber camps. His mother, Clara, known to nearly everyone as Dot, ran a boarding house for the workers. Clara died when Frank was nine, leaving him and his father to fend for themselves. Frank's three older brothers had already left home by that time.

After a year or so, Thomas Pratt took off for Seattle, leaving Frank to be raised by his mother's sister, Aunt Bess, who also lived in Blanchard. For the next few years Frank divided his time between Aunt Bess and his brother, Loren, in Bellingham, Washington. He graduated from Fairhaven High School and later attended Western Washington State College.

Music was always important to Frank, and as a young man he spent a lot of Saturday nights at the local dancehall. He liked the bass fiddle best and if he wasn't dancing he would stand in front of the stage and watch. Apparently this caught the attention of the bass player, and the two men eventually struck up a conversation. At the end of one evening the bass player asked if Frank would like to borrow his fiddle. "Sure!" Frank said. He didn't have a car, but he found a way to get the instrument home. He taught himself to play by strumming along with the radio and favorite phonograph records. The dancehall musician never asked to have his fiddle returned, but he passed Frank's name along to a local bandleader. One day Frank got a call from a man named Clarence Barney who was looking for a replacement bass player for the coming Saturday night. Frank was mighty nervous playing his first real gig, but he must have passed the test, since Charles Barney and the band asked him back to play the following Saturday, and the one after that. Soon he was a full-fledged member of the group. Over the next decade he played steadily with local swing bands, until he was inducted into the military in 1943. He returned to playing after coming home from the war and finally hung up his bass for good in the late 1950s.

Along with his fiddle playing, Frank worked for a number of years in the service station business and eventually owned two stations of his own.

When World War II started, Frank was interested in joining the Army Air Corps as an officer candidate. He enlisted in the fall of 1942, just before his twenty-seventh birthday, and was sent to San Angelo Army Airfield, Texas, one of four Army Air Forces fields collectively known as the West Texas Bombardier Quadrangle. He graduated at the end of 1943 as a bombardier with the rank of 2nd Lieutenant, and in March 1944, he and his fellow B-24 crew members were assigned to the European theater. They arrived there in the spring of 1944, after flying their B-24 across the Atlantic via Brazil and North Africa. From April 20, Frank and his crew were stationed in Venosa, Italy, as members of the 831st Squadron, part of the 485th Bombardment Group of the Fifteenth Air Force. ("Life in Combat Theater begins! Hooray.")

By fall of 1944, Frank's regular unit had flown all of the fifty missions required to complete their tour of duty, and most of the men returned to the U.S. However Frank developed an ear infection that grounded him for a couple of weeks. After this he was obliged to fly make-up missions with other crews. He was still completing these when he was shot down on September 13, 1944, over southern Poland, near Wadowice, about twenty miles from Krakau. It was Frank's forty-third mission. His B-24 was hit by flak. Five of the crew members parachuted out; six didn't make it.

When Frank landed he was picked up by a pitchfork-wielding German on a motorcycle and taken prisoner. Over the next few days he was interrogated and taken by train from Poland through central Germany to a transient camp in Frankfurt. There he was assigned and sent by train once again to Stalag Luft I, a permanent POW camp for American and British air officers on a peninsula near the Baltic Sea town of Barth, Germany.

Shortly after arriving at Stalag Luft I, Frank started keeping a diary. Some of his barracks mates did the same, in part because there wasn't much else to do and writing was a good way to pass the time. Paper, however, was fairly hard to come by. One day as Frank was sitting in his barracks it occurred to him that the empty cigarette packs strewn across the floor were made of fairly heavy stock that was blank on one side, and if he trimmed off the torn edges and cut them to a uniform size, they would make good writing paper. So the "cigarette diaries" came to be.

The Three Diaries: *The first two journals (at left) have cardboard covers cut from Red Cross parcel boxes that are sewn together at the top with canvas, probably from a mattress cover. Inside, they contain journal entries written in pencil on the backs of flattened and trimmed cigarette packs. The third and last journal is a traditional "blue book," a slightly larger, paper-covered blue notebook that was supplied to POWs by the YMCA.*

Preface

Like many people of his generation, my father, Frank Pratt, was uncomfortable having too much attention focused on him. In all the years I was growing up and living at home, I almost never heard him talk about his being in the war or in prison camp. If the subject ever came up, he was quick to tell people who suggested he was a hero that he was just doing his job, and that there were hundreds of thousands of GIs who were all heroes. I remember him taking my mom and me to see the movie *The Great Escape* when I was a child, but even while my parents talked about it in the car on the way home afterwards I still had no idea that my Dad had spent eight months in a POW camp like the one in the movie.

Dad first showed me his diaries in 1994, when he and the rest of his B-24 crew who were shot down over Poland were honored by the Polish government in a medals ceremony in Washington D.C. I had never known the diaries existed until then, but from the first time I saw them, I was fascinated and wanted to transcribe and somehow preserve them. There were three books. Two were made of bound cigarette wrappers; the third, which contains longer entries, was a "blue book" (journals supplied to POWs by the YMCA that had blue paper covers). Together they document the eight months of my Dad's time as a POW. One section in Book II also recounts his crew's adventures on their journey from the U.S. to their home base in Venosa, Italy when they were first sent overseas.

When my employer, *Newsweek* Magazine, decided in 2007 to run an article about Ken Burns' epic WWII television series, *The War*, I convinced my Dad to let me show the diaries to one of my editors. They jumped at the chance to do a piece about them and produced a three-part video interview with my father that ran on the *Newsweek* website along with excerpts from the diaries. That was enough to motivate me to get going and transcribe all three books.

I tried to stay as true to the originals as possible, using my father's spellings, abbreviations, etc. Because the writing was very faint in some spots and my father's handwriting could be tough to decipher—even he was stumped by some of it—there were a few words that were impossible to figure out. In those cases, I either made my best guess based on context or left a question mark.

Once I had finished all three journals I decided the best thing to do was to turn them into a book. The first edition was published privately as a small hardcover volume in 2008. The process of bringing this about was entirely a labor of love, and I felt lucky to have had the chance to get to know more about my father as a young man. The diaries made me laugh, they made me cry and, best of all, they made me feel much, much closer to my Dad. I was proud to be able to surprise him with a copy of the printed version before he died in 2008.

In 2015, I was approached by Réanne Hemingway-Douglass, of Cave Art Press, about publishing a new edition of *The Cigarette Diaries*. Réanne had chanced upon a copy of the book several years earlier, and felt it deserved wider readership. She was struck by the suspenseful quality of the later entries, as the POWs monitored the daily Allied gains and took bets on the date of their eventual liberation; by my father's droll humor and humanity (making fudge in response to the news on May 3, 1945, that the newly-liberated POWs might fly out within the next forty-eight hours); and by the fact that the diaries overall tell "a really good story that is part of history."

Réanne and her staff proposed a number of changes to my original—verbatim—transcripts of the diaries. Their efforts clarified some of the more obscure entries, added context, and improved the readability. My father's words have been preserved as far as possible, but his note-like entries have been expanded into a more readable narrative, and some material has been re-arranged to reflect the actual chronology of events.

Additional historical information has been added where it was felt to be editorially appropriate. Much of it was sourced from the article 'Downed Aircraft Over Europe: Revival of Polish Affection at the End of the Cold War,' by military historian Daniel R. Mortenson, published in the journal *Air Power History*, Spring 1993, and the book *Don't Let the Blue Star Turn Gold – Downed Airmen in Europe in WWII*, by Jerry

W. Whiting (Tarnaby Press, Walnut Creek, CA, 2003). Both of these authors conducted telephone interviews with my father and other surviving crewmembers of the B-24 that was shot down over Osweicim, Poland, on September 13, 1944. Additional information was obtained from www.485thbg.org, a website maintained by the 485th Bomb Group Association and dedicated to the men who served with the 485th Bombardment Group in Venosa, Italy, during World War II. Other sources are acknowledged in the text. Arlene Cook, who did most of the editorial work on the book, accepts responsibility for any factual errors.

I am grateful to Réanne, Arlene, and their Cave Art Press colleagues Kathleen Kaska and Lisa Wright for their interest in this project and the work they have put into it. I also remain grateful to *Newsweek*, and especially to website videographer Jonathan Groat, for the wonderful interviews with my Dad that got me started on the transcription process; to Rose Unes, without whose help the original book might never have made it to press, and to David Olivenbaum, who enthusiastically proofread the diary entries and graciously and skillfully edited my small contributions to this work. Thank you, also, to all of my colleagues and friends who encouraged me and helped me to make this happen, and to Bernice Pratt, whose support and encouragement helped my Dad feel comfortable enough to share his war experiences and his diaries.

Above all, I wish to thank my father, Frank Pratt, who will always remain my hero.

Rebecca Pratt
Blanchard, Washington
May, 2016

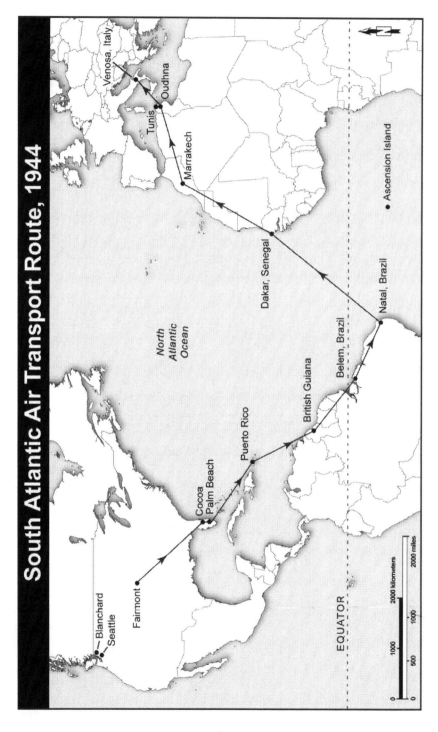

South Atlantic Air Transport Route, 1944

Starting out

The following is an edited version of an entry that appears in Book II of the original Cigarette Diaries. *Chronologically, however, this is the beginning of the story, as it refers to the journey made in the spring of 1944 by Frank Pratt, his original B-24 crew, and the rest of the 831st Bomb Squadron from their base in the U.S. to the European combat theater. Frank referred to the various stops along the way only by their initials, but he offers enough clues to suggest that the B-24s followed the standard South Atlantic transport route for four-engine aircraft of the World War II era, flying south to the easternmost point in Brazil and taking the "big hop" from there across the Atlantic to West Africa.*

March 11 – April 20, 1944

Took off from L. [?Lincoln, Nebraska/Fairmont Army Airfield], 8:15 a.m. Saturday, March 11. Cold and tired after only two hours of sleep. Lots of last minute packing and running around. Headed south. I went to sleep and woke up to see the [Mississippi] river. Bad weather from then on—snow and ice—and our radio went out, so we missed our destination [Naval Air Station Banana River, now Patrick Air Force Base, Cocoa, Florida]. Buzzed C. [Cocoa] below the water tower. No help. Gas low. Willie [assumed to be the navigator, Wilbur Hyman] was positive we were only short ways off. Getting dark. 500 foot ceiling. Chutes on, hatch open. Engineer said to take 'er up. Spotted an airfield under construction; we'd passed over it an hour before. Made approach and landed. Quick thinking by our pilot avoided disaster—the 2000-foot runway was not finished, and tractors and bulldozers took up half of it. Everybody was pretty nervous, since we only had about 200 feet of runway left, and it was raining hard. But lady luck was with us.

Walked over to the watchman's hut. What a character. After much discussion he took us to the nearest town. This was C. [Cocoa], a small Navy town which we had buzzed. The weather cleared and became very warm and balmy. We were still in our heavy flying suits, which attracted some curious looks. We made the necessary phone calls and finally found rooms at the Indian River Hotel. Pretty swanky. After washing up a bit and removing flying clothing we visited a little night spot. I had an oyster dinner and several shots of bourbon, which quieted my nerves. Slept well.

Fooled around the hotel admiring the landscape and view until about 1 p.m., when we left for the ship [the crew's B-24]. The shore police were very kind. A better look at the airfield in daylight showed us how lucky we were. A major from M. [either Miami or Morrison Field, Palm Beach, Florida] flew in to look over the situation. One runway was almost finished, but when measured it was not quite long enough. The contractor bulldozed out 500 feet more and felled some trees at the end. Then we were ready to go. Several hundred people gathered to watch. We took off and just cleared the trees. The tail skid scared me when it came up. We nearly got lost again. After hours we arrived at our destination. Our navigation had really been off!

At M. [Morrison Field] we spent three days having work done on the ship and taking care of last minute details. It was a large airfield but we were not allowed off it. However, we saw the surrounding country from the air on our way in—really swanky!

Took off, with pigeons, about 2:30 a.m. By daylight we were well out over the ocean. The ship was using excessive gas, so we decided to stop at P. [Puerto Rico], where we landed at about 1200 hours. This was the nicest airfield of the trip, with beautiful weather, modern buildings, cheap liquor and good food. The crew made several test flights. I goofed off on all of 'em and went to the beach or the bar. The slot machines were generous, the PX girls cute, and I enjoyed all four of the days we spent there. But we had trouble with a runaway propeller when we took off, and had to return. Finally got going by 0900 hours.

Arrived at G. [British Guiana] at about 1600 hours. This was not so nice as the last field and the weather was much hotter and stickier. The ship was still giving trouble, so we did some more test hops. We stayed there for three days. The liquor was still cheap but the food and barracks were not so good. Monday was movie night. On Tuesday there was a dance, with native girls from town and a few nurses and WAC [Women's Army Corps] officers. It was not much larger than a private party. I tagged after the native girls, but they were rather aloof. I walked around a lot, but there was not much to see but wilderness. Despite this, I goofed off on flying the test hops. Jake [2nd Lt. Theodore 'Ted' Jacobs, pilot] was still not satisfied with the ship but nothing could be done about it there. I can't remember the takeoff. I must have been awful sleepy or had a hangover.

Next stop B. [Belem, Brazil]. Really nasty flying weather—1000-foot ceiling and raining like hell. We passed over jungle and the last hour over the big river [i.e., the Amazon]. Really huge. We flew over it at about 300 feet. Belem, although modern, was awful sloppy, wet and hot, with an awful smell everywhere that was said to be jungle rot. The food tasted of it too. Native girls working in the mess hall were very flirtatious. The small officers' club was very bad. Canadian Club whiskey cost $8.00 a quart, with no ice, no mixer, no water. We only stayed overnight there, and took off about 0600 the next morning for N. [Natal, Brazil], the last place before the big hop across the Atlantic.

We really saw the jungle on this leg of the trip—a green mass. Landed at Natal about at 1400 hours. It was hot and dusty and large, but a modern field, with nice barracks and a fair officers' Club. There was a big day room and a fair mess also, although it was usually too hot to be enjoyable. We did lots of test hops here, and drew per diem pay. I got awful stinko on a couple of nights, which amused Willie and Bob [2nd Lt. Robert Hanna, co-pilot]. I also saw my first outdoor movie. I bought some Chanel #5 and mosquito boots. Lots of fellows here bought silk stockings and watches, but these didn't look like such good bargains to me. I went down to the beach once. Native women were selling everything, I mean…! Beautiful water and sand, however, and a cool breeze.

We had a big argument with Operations over the route we should take across the Atlantic. Jake and Willie claimed we couldn't make D. [Dakar, Senegal, 1,876 miles from Natal], and wanted to go by A. [Ascension Island, 1,438 miles]. The major gave detailed instructions and said they wouldn't fail. Jake took a vote among the crew and we decided to try it. We were scheduled to take off at 0200, but the ship wasn't ready. By 0400, we were ready to go. Then a bomb bay door fell off. It was repaired, and we finally took off at 0600. There wasn't much to see after that, just lots of water. Willie caused some excitement seven hours out when he said we had seven hours left to go and only five hours' worth of gas. But he righted his mistake, much to our relief. We landed twelve hours and five minutes after taking off. This was our first landing on a steel mat, and we thought from the noise that everything had gone haywire. A dip at end of the runway was deceiving also. The oddest thing, though, was that we had plenty of gas left. The boy at Natal was definitely right. ["Boy" is not used here in a derogatory sense. Airmen routinely referred to one another as "boys."]

In Dakar we got our first sight of Lebanese [Senegalese?] guards. They were quite the boys for build and bright colors. The airfield was really dusty and a long way from barracks. The food was definitely not good, nor was anything else, and it was hotter'n blazes. We had to line up in the PX for Cokes and ice cream, and the officers' club served mostly wine. We were allowed to go to the beach here in a G.I. truck. En route we passed through a small town, which was my first introduction to real filth and begging kids. There were a couple of dead camels and a goat nobody seemed to bother about. Truck drivers had difficulty driving through the mobs of kids and men begging for cigarettes. It was really a desolate place, very sloppy and dusty. Malaria was bad all along our route so far, but it was worse here. Saw bad crack-up remains, learned more of it later. Fortunately we stayed only two days.

Took off from Dakar about 0800, arrived at M. [Marrakech, French Morocco] about 1400. The trip to M. was exciting a couple of times. Once we were almost into a neutral country [either Spanish Morocco or Spanish Sahara, now Western Sahara]; the second time we had trouble over the Atlas Mountains. One other crew had bad luck on their hop [B-24 pilot Robert Olney and his crew were killed when their aircraft struck a mountain]. There were no landmarks to speak of, only sand and now and then a little bunch grass. The field at Marrakech was crowded and we had a long wait to check in. Then we were assigned to our quarters—little run down shacks with cots, two blankets, and candle light. I was pretty gloomy and blue by the time I got settled so I cracked a bottle of Old Crow and sat up 'til the wee hours nipping at it and thinking.

We had a pass to town the next day. Bob and I started out hitchin' but didn't have much luck. Finally we caught trucks that Jake and Willie were on. This was our first look at a foreign city and French women—not bad! There were sidewalk bars, also peddlers and beggars. Prices were high and things were not too sanitary. We spent the time sight-seeing and window shopping. The residential district was nice. The Medina [souk or bazaar] was off limits, but we heard a wild story of two majors masquerading as Arabs and going in there. Later we found out they were two guys from our outfit [831st Bombardment Squadron].

After another test hop, we left for our final destination the next day. This was Oodna [Oudhna, Tunisia], where we arrived on April 3. Life really began anew! We moved into our tent, bag and baggage. It was good to see all the boys again, though things were in a mess and everything was pretty dirty and dusty. There were long mess lines for food cooked on homemade stoves. Eventually we moved to a new site that had a little more organization.

A trip to T. [Tunis] to see the sights. I was AWOL for a couple days. Too much vermouth, and I missed last truck to base on purpose. Tunis was not too safe after dark. A blackout was in force and I had a hard time with a hotel clerk. This resulted in a mix up with a city marshal and some other jerk. After this I moved out of my room to one at the Hotel Atlantique.

**

Sent to Italy on April 20th. Life in Combat Theater begins! Hooray.

Frank Pratt (in front, second from right) with his original crewmates and their "ship," the Flak-Shak II, in Venosa, Italy, July, 1944. Pilot Theodore Jacobs, co-pilot Robert Hanna, navigator Wilbur Hyman, bombardier Frank Pratt, radio gunner Leo O'Brien, engineer-gunner Joe South, upper gunner Leroy Hoffheins, ball gunner John Koch, tail gunner William Roy, and nose gunner James Sowers were all awarded the Distinguished Flying Cross for aiding and escorting a damaged bomber back to home base while returning from a harrowing mission over Vienna on June 16, 1944.

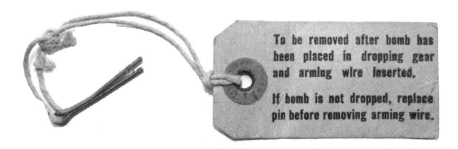

Shot Down

The information in this section is derived from the article 'Downed Aircraft Over Europe: Revival of Polish Affection at the End of the Cold War,' by Daniel R. Mortensen, Don't Let the Blue Star Turn Gold – Downed Airmen in Europe in WWII, *by Jerry W. Whiting, and the website www.485thbg.org.*

Venosa, Italy, was home to the 485th Bombardment Group, one of twenty-one such groups assigned to the U.S. Fifteenth Air Force. The airfield was new when Frank Pratt and his B-24 crewmates arrived in April 1944, with only one permanent building—an old farm house—on the entire base. Aircrews were housed in tents, although additional facilities were constructed as the months progressed. The field was five miles from the village of Venosa, in southern Italy, and sixty miles from the headquarters of the Fifteenth Air Force at Bari, on the Adriatic coast.

The 485th Group was comprised of four Squadrons of B-24 heavy bombers, each of which numbered twelve or more aircraft. Frank Pratt and his crew were members of the 831st Squadron, led by Captain Daniel Sjoden. Bombing operations were conducted in part according to a strategy devised in March 1944 by General Carl Spaatz, Commander of Strategic Air Forces in Europe, to disrupt German oil production by targeting refineries and other oil facilities in Germany, Austria, Czechoslovakia and the Balkans. Missions flown by 485th Group bombers included raids on refineries in Ploesti (Romania), Smerdervo (Yugoslavia), Petfurdo (Hungary) and Vienna (Austria), interspersed with attacks on aircraft manufacturing plants, chemical factories, harbor facilities, and railway marshalling yards. By the end of August, 1944, the Ploesti oilfields in Romania had been overrun by the advancing Russian Army, but the oil disruption campaign continued as bombing missions were directed towards new targets further afield.

Official records indicate that approximately 3500 men served in the 485th Bomb Group in Venosa, including at least 2500 air crew. They flew 187 missions out of Venosa between May 10, 1944, and April 25,

1945, dropping 10,550 tons of bombs on enemy installations and destroying or damaging as many as 100 enemy aircraft. Fifty-nine bombers from the 485th Group were lost in combat; sixty-two others were involved in accidents or were salvaged as a result of combat. At least 475 men were killed in combat or died from combat injuries. Approximately 250 airmen—including Frank Pratt and four of his crewmates—became POWs. Thirteen men who were captured managed to escape and made their way safely back to Italy. A further 140 men who were shot down managed to evade capture altogether, and they, too, returned safely.

September 13, 1944

On September 13, 1944—the day Frank Pratt was shot down—the 485th Group's target was the Oswiecim (Auschwitz) synthetic oil and rubber plant, in southern Poland. During the pre-flight briefing, the mission leader, Lt. Col. Bill Herblin, pointed out the large "labor camp" near the plant, and warned his bombardiers to avoid dropping their bombs on it. If Herblin or his Air Force superiors were aware of the atrocities being committed at the camp, they did not share this information with the flight crews.

The Osweicim target had been bombed by B-17s from the Fifteenth Air Force a month previously, but the B-24 crews on this day were told that anti-aircraft fire would probably be light. However, the mission required that they make their longest flight yet from Venosa, most of it over enemy-held territory. For this reason it was deemed to be sufficiently dangerous to be worth two mission credits towards the fifty each crewman needed to complete before being rotated back to the States.

All missions, including this one, were cause for anxiety, but on this particular day the crew of Frank Pratt's B-24 were unusually nervous. Although the men all knew one another, most had not flown together on a regular basis. They were a "made-up" crew of volunteers from other B-24s who, for various reasons, had not flown as many missions as other members of their original crews. In Frank Pratt's case, he had been grounded for two weeks with an ear infection. The September 13 mission would be his forty-third; most of his regular crewmates, who had all flown together since before their departure for Italy, had already completed their requisite fifty missions and were on their way home. Frank had been flying almost daily since returning to his squadron, filling in for any crews who needed a bombardier. At twenty-eight, he was older than most of the men he flew with, but almost all of them were seasoned mission veterans.

For several of the make-up crew, including the pilot, Captain William C. Lawrence, the Osweicim mission would be their fiftieth bombing run. Lawrence had an excellent reputation as a pilot, and co-pilots routinely asked to fly with him, but everyone was superstitious about final missions. The date—the 13th—was considered unlucky also. Of additional, practical concern to Lawrence was the fact that he would be flying a new, untried ship, a silver B-24J that lacked the drab green camouflage of his usual plane, the Hell's Angel, which was undergoing repairs. The new aircraft was referred to as a "mickey ship," because it had a radar unit in place of the ball turret on the underside of the fuselage.

Other crew members besides Lawrence (pilot) and Frank Pratt (bombardier) were:

First Lieutenant Matthew W. Hall (co-pilot)
Second Lieutenant Daniel N. Blodgett (1st navigator)
First Lieutenant George V. Winter (2nd navigator)
Second Lieutenant Irving Canin (3rd radar navigator)
Technical Sergeant Everett L. MacDonald (engineer)
Technical Sergeant William T. Eggers (radio operator)
Staff Sergeant Arthur E. Nitsche (rear gunner)
Staff Sergeant Lewis L. Kaplan (waist gunner)
Staff Sergeant Vernon O. Christensen (top turret gunner)

MacDonald, Nitsche and Christensen were members of Lawrence's Hell's Angel crew and, like him, they were flying their fiftieth mission. Winter and Eggers, though they had come from different crews, were also on their fiftieth mission. Three navigators were aboard because Lawrence's B-24 was designated as one of the lead aircraft on the mission and required a radar navigator, and Blodgett was in training as a lead navigator.

The aircraft took off from Venosa at 0615 hours with twenty-seven other B-24s from the 485th Bomber Group. Off the east coast of Italy they joined eighty-nine other B-24s from three additional groups, together with P-38 and P-51 fighters which escorted them as far as Yugoslavia. Thirteen bombers experienced mechanical problems and turned back; the rest continued on to Poland. Lawrence's crew sang and joked with one another to ease their nerves and pass the time.

Flying at 20,000 feet, the bombers reached Osweicim at around 1100 hours. The target area was obscured both by clouds and by camouflage smoke generated by the Germans, so the bombardiers followed directions supplied by the radar navigator, Irving Canin.

In spite of the assurances given at the pre-flight briefing, "surprisingly heavy flak" burst forth ahead of the aircraft. As they reached the IP—the Initial Point, at which they were to begin the straight, level run to drop their bombs—it got closer. Aboard Lawrence's ship, Vernon Christensen, the top turret gunner, left his station to put his parachute in a place where he could get to it quickly if needed. As he climbed back into his turret the plane took a direct hit in the right wing, causing the third engine to burst into flames.

Frank Pratt felt the aircraft shudder moments after he dropped his bombs. He exchanged a worried glance with George Winter, one of the navigators, who shared his forward compartment. The bomber dropped out of formation and into a slow downward spiral. Winter could see that the pilots were unable to regain control of the plane and realized they would have to abandon ship. No alarm sounded to indicate this but Vernon Christensen, who had a clear view of the damaged wing from his forward turret, yelled into the intercom: "The engine is on fire. We've gotta get out!"

Winter and Pratt did so by lowering the nose wheel and jumping through the opening. Three other crew members—Christensen, Blodgett and Canin—exited out of the bomb bay. Moments after this the aircraft went into a spin. None of the six men remaining aboard were able to bail out because of centrifugal forces that pinned them against the inside of the fuselage.

The aircraft broke up in the air, scattering burning pieces of wreckage over the ground and killing a young woman, Maria Opalinski. She had been plowing a field with her father when the bombers appeared overhead. One plane seemed likely to crash on top of them. The engines separated from the wing and one fell between Maria and her father. She was badly burned and died twelve days later.

As they descended by parachute, none of the surviving airmen knew where in Poland they were about to land. Some thought their plane had continued to fly northwards from Osweicim, others that it had turned south after dropping its load of bombs. In fact, they were about twenty miles south-east of the target area, near the village of Wadowice, twenty-five miles south-west of Krakau.

George Winter saw as he parachuted downwards from 20,000 feet that he was going to land in an area of open farmland. There would be little possibility of escape, so he discarded his service pistol before he hit the ground to reduce the chances of being shot during capture. A German patrol drove up after he landed. Winter surrendered to them and was driven to a building in a nearby village [Wadowice], where he was physically searched and asked by an interrogator for his name, rank and serial number.

Vernon Christensen had suffered from an interruption to his oxygen supply while still aboard the aircraft and was battling grogginess. His crewmates helped him to put on his parachute and bail out. His arms were burned and he became rapidly chilled as he was wearing neither his flying helmet nor his heavy sheepskin flying boots. He landed among villagers, but a soldier arrived quickly, and indicated that he should put his hands up and surrender his pistol. Christensen did not have a weapon, but he had two cigarettes and gave one to the soldier. He was in shock from the bail out and the long, cold descent, and remembered little of what happened next, beyond being reunited with his four surviving crewmates and spending the night in a town building.

Daniel Blodgett, the 1st navigator, who had helped Christensen out of the aircraft before bailing out himself, fell for a long time before his parachute opened. He remembered seeing parachutes above and below him, and that his descent was very quiet until some dogs started barking as he approached the ground. An enemy soldier greeted him as he landed, and instructed him to "uppen hands."

Irving Canin, the radio navigator, was the last man to escape from the plane. He told Blodgett when the men were reunited that evening that he had barely managed to get out because of the centrifugal forces arising from the spin. Lawrence and Hall, the pilots, had been preparing to exit behind him, but had been trapped inside the plane.

Frank Pratt, the bombardier, had a problematic descent. Seconds before the aircraft had been hit, he had unbuckled the leg hook on his parachute harness so he could use the relief tube [a funnel-shaped urination device]. He had failed to reattach the leg hook afterwards, so the parachute was only partially attached to the harness during his descent. Fearing he might fall through the harness, Pratt hung onto the straps "for dear life." He recalled hearing "whizzing noises"—gun shots—around him as he approached the ground, but he landed safely, and about ten minutes later a soldier and a civilian drove up in a sidecar and he was instructed to climb aboard.

Frank Pratt in Venosa, Italy, August 1944. The markings on his flight jacket indicate thirty-six completed missions. He was shot down on his 43rd mission. The hand-written inscription reads Greetings from the Roman Candle, "Franko."

14

BOOK I

Sept. 13/44.

Landed in Poland at approx
1115. Captured at 1120 — by civilians & jerry Soldiers about 60
of them. Mistook Soldiers
for Poles - very friendly. Removed from field, where I landed,
to a city hall in some small
village. Rode in Motorcycle
sidecar - Six others picked on.
Taken into room, evidently civil
police station. George is there
along with some poorly dressed
Soldiers. Seem to be arguing
about what to do with us. Numerous telephone calls. Finally take
our electric equip. away from
us. Try to talk to us in German.
No luck. Are Removed to a
Small Room & placed under
guard.

Captured

September 13, 1944

Landed in Poland at approximately 11:15, captured at 11:20 [a.m.] by civilians and Jerry soldiers, about sixty of them in all. The soldiers were very friendly and I mistook them for Poles. They took me in a motorcycle sidecar, with about six other people piled on, to a city hall in a small village. I was taken into a room that was evidently the police station. George [Winter, 2nd navigator] was there too, together with some poorly dressed soldiers who were arguing, presumably about what they should do with us. They made numerous telephone calls and finally took our electrical equipment away from us. They tried to talk to us in German, but without luck. George and I were removed to a small room and placed under guard.

We were taken out of the room again and searched. Three more members of our crew had been brought in by then, and we were moved as a group to a larger town to the south. We were taken before a Jerry major, a captain, and a private who served as interpreter. They made it clear that we were not in friendly hands. More silly questions were asked, more telephone calls made. The interpreter told us we would be shot if we didn't talk. But we all kept quiet. Eventually we were taken back outside where a crowd of at least 500 people had gathered. The Major ordered us to line up against a wall and he took pictures of each of us. The civilians were friendly, but they were pushed roughly away.

We were taken by bus to Krakau and arrived there at six o'clock. Krakau appeared as a large city with little evidence of bomb damage. Confusion still reigned where we were concerned, and our driver was evidently lost. We stopped for an hour at some kind of military headquarters, then moved on towards the sun [i.e., west], arriving at dusk at what appeared to be a sanitarium, about six miles out of Krakau. There, we were given our first food for the day—German bread and ersatz coffee. After this we were taken to a gym that had been turned into a guardhouse. Eight Russian pilots were already there. They were badly burned. At about 9 p.m. the Major and the interpreter came in and we were relieved of our shoes and pants. I was severely bawled out for whistling in the Major's presence. We were issued two blankets and instructed to go to sleep on the floor. About twenty guards with machine pistols kept watch over us, the lights remained on all night, and the floor was hard and cold. The Russians had been given hay as bedding and offered us some of it. The German guards refused to interact with us in any way. We had no cigarettes and got little sleep.

September 14

Breakfast was ersatz coffee and two slices of black bread. The Russians slipped us some Polish cigarettes, which wasn't much but better than nothing. A navigator [Blodgett or Canin] attempted to talk French to the Jerries but he asked silly questions and the rest of us grew bored. We had good food at noon—a boiled dinner, and plenty of it, which really hit the spot. After this we were allowed to go out in the sunshine, which eased the stiffness from our previous day's experiences. Plenty of guards watched over us. The Russians were not allowed out. One German, a former taxi driver in New York City, tried to engage us in conversation, but without luck. We were given our first cigarette rations—five per day—and informed that we would be moving tomorrow. The Russians told us in sign language that we were twenty miles from the Russian front. There seemed no chance for escape.

September 15

We didn't move after all, but spent most of the afternoon outside and felt a little better for it. The Russians were moved, however. As they filed out, each of them shook hands with us. This was against the rules but felt really sincere, particularly as their fate according to the Jerries would not be good. [As Daniel Mortenson notes, American POWs were treated better than Russians; air officers were treated better than ground officers;

and officers were treated better than enlisted men. The Russians in this instance were reported by a German soldier to have been taken out and shot.]

We talked over our situation and wondered about the rest of our crew. We decided that Lawrence and Hall had either escaped or did not get out of the plane. The latter seemed most likely. Five survivors out of eleven is not so good.

A German fighter pilot—a captain—talked to us and said the war would last another six months. We smiled. Maybe he was right.

September 16

We left Krakau with four guards, marching two miles to a train and carrying our rations for the next twenty-four hours—a loaf of bread, margarine (lard), a small sausage, half a can of fish, and five cigarettes.

En route through the city we stopped at a German first aid station, where my finger and a boil on my neck were bandaged. We had a short-arm inspection also! The people in Krakau appeared indifferent to us. Several times we tried mingling among soldiers and civilians, out of sight of our guards, but it seemed like a poor place to escape.

We boarded the train and were put in a car with several compartments, four men and two guards to each one. About twenty-five other Americans were already aboard. I hoped the rest of the crew might be among them, but no such luck. We left at dark. Sleep was difficult as the seats were very hard and we made numerous stops through the night. Outside, everything was blacked out.

September 17

I woke up feeling pretty weary after a bad night aboard the train. We passed three pretty farming communities, and through Schweinfurt and Leipzig. Both cities were a mess from the bombings. It was also upsetting to see the tangled mass of a plane, evidently a B-17, beside the tracks. Our guards told us that our destination would be Frankfurt, and they warned us not to smile, talk or laugh when we left the train. Otherwise, the guards were pretty good sports about us bothering them, as we asked them to cut our bread, go to the can, etc. Jerry soldiers who boarded the train were less good humored, as they had to sit in the aisles while we occupied the compartments. The train was delayed, also, because some of the tracks had been blown up, and we had to change trains several times.

We arrived in Frankfurt about 11 p.m., then marched about three miles through mist and rain to a Dulag. [Dulag is an abbreviation of Durchgangslager der Luftwaffe—a transit camp for captured Allied air forces personnel. The Dulag in this instance was at Oberursel, outside of Frankfurt. It was used by the Germans throughout the war as a major collection and interrogation center for newly captured aircrews.]

No one we passed seemed friendly, but it was an even more unpleasant shock to get our first glimpse of spotlights, barbed wire and real stockades. Nor were we treated kindly. We were searched, our shoes were taken away, and we were placed in solitary confinement. I was feeling pretty gloomy and tired by then, and didn't give much of a damn about anything.

September 18

We were awakened at 8 a.m. for breakfast: bread and coffee. I took careful note of my room. It was square, about eight feet by eight feet. The bed was a dirty blanket and a sack that leaked straw. The only other item was a glass jar; I had drunk coffee out of it, but closer examination made me wonder what else it had been used for. The single window was of the opaque sort. Numerous marks on the walls denoted days spent in the cell by previous occupants. One stretch amounted to twenty-seven days—and I was already getting nervous after a single night.

To go to the latrine I had to turn a knob, which raised a signal flag in the hallway. The guards took anything from ten to fifty minutes to respond. Funny how a craving to be alone fades when solitude is forced upon you. Time dragged. We had barley soup for lunch, bread and coffee again at night. After that: no light, no heat, and fleas. I feel a little PO'd.

September 19

A repeat of the previous day, until noon, when I was photographed and interrogated. Pretty tricky, these Jerries, but I enjoyed being out of the hole for a while. At 4 p.m. I was told to get ready to move. This made me really happy. I was then placed in a compound with about a hundred other men, who would presumably be moving with me. Meanwhile, I could walk outside until dusk and talk again to somebody. Freedom, although limited, is a great thing.

September 20

Up early, 5:30 a.m., ready to leave by 7 a.m. A march of about a mile back to the station. People shook their fists and made throat-slicing gestures, which made us feel guilty and gave us an unpleasant sense of their city. We were actually grateful for the numerous guards. Our next stop was to be another transient camp, reportedly about an hour's journey away. Four hours later we arrived at Wetzlar. More marching, this time uphill to a camp.

Despite the barbed wire it seemed relatively cheerful and we were glad to get there. None of us had shaved or bathed for a week, and I'm sure we appeared to be a pretty sad lot. More questions, then we were issued with Red Cross suitcases. What a feeling! Then came a hot shower, the first real food for some time, plenty of cigarettes, and a song fest in the evening. A few guys shed tears. The officer in charge, a full colonel, was a real kick in the pants. He said Wetzlar was known as the country club of prison camps. How true.

The Wetzlar camp was a satellite of the Oberursal Dulag. It was established later in the war to help process the increasing numbers of aircrews who were shot down as the Allied bombing campaign against Germany intensified.

We spent four days in the Wetzlar camp. During this time there were at least seven air raids, the most memorable of which was at least three hours long. I could sympathize with the civilians, as it wasn't fun being in a shelter for long. Two raids came at night after we were in bed. On the second day a big factory about a mile away was hit. Only one squadron dropped their bombs but the concussion was great—and everybody was happy, darkly so, because the bombs didn't fall in the middle of camp. Ships at 20,000 feet are pretty small. After every raid a couple of [Messerschmitt] 109s would take off bravely and fly around at 5,000 feet.

We had good food all the time we were at Wetzlar, with extra cocoa and biscuits at about 8 p.m. every evening, which everybody appreciated. There was music and singing every night, too—along with very inaccurate news reports. Altogether there were about 300 POWs, English and American. All were Air Corps, enlisted men and officers, who were segregated and sent on to permanent camps. Christensen, our top turret gunner and the only enlisted man in our crew, left us here. New POWs came in every day. A navigator, Canin, whom we had left behind at the flea hole [Oberursal], arrived just as we were leaving. The Colonel told us our C.O., who was shot down in July, came in also; he was wounded badly but is doing okay. I didn't see anybody else I knew.

Frank apparently wrote this account from memory several months after the events he describes had transpired. Daniel Mortenson writes that Vernon Christensen, a sergeant, was separated from his crewmates, who were all officers, in Wadowice the day after their capture. He was eventually sent to Stalag Luft IV, a camp for enlisted men in Poland, where conditions were particularly miserable.

The "C.O." is presumed to have been Colonel Walter P. Arnold, the first commander of the 485th Bombardment Group, who was shot down over Blechhammer, in what is now southern Poland, on August 27, 1944. Badly wounded in the leg, Arnold was interrogated at Oberursal after a period of hospitalization. He passed through the Wetzlar Dulag before being sent to Stalag Luft III in Sagan, Poland. The dates of his transfers, as reported by the 485th Bomb Group Association, do not fit with Frank Pratt's account, but Arnold's story matches descriptively.

September 24

One hundred and twenty of us left Wetzlar on this day. Four wounded men who were unable to walk were taken by bus to the train station. The rest of us, after being warned by Jerry guards about trying to escape, marched down to the train. We looked a little better than the day we arrived, and we were in much better spirits.

At about 7 p.m. we were loaded into POW coaches with barred windows, ten men to each eight-man compartment. This was uncomfortable but it was destined to get worse. Our compartment was cold and smoky. We were not allowed to open the windows. After an hour, the train began to move, but only to a siding where we spent the rest of the night. We had a helluva time getting to sleep. I tried the baggage racks, the floor, and sitting up, all without much success.

September 25

At nine o'clock we were each issued a Red Cross parcel, and the train finally got moving. We proceeded at a snail's pace all day. There was lots of wreckage from bombing and we stopped in marshalling yards for long periods. We expected to be bombed or strafed by our Allies at any moment. By 7 p.m. we had covered about twenty-five miles. Conditions in the car were getting pretty bad. We were so crowded, and the latrine was deplorable.

September 26

We made better time today, but the car was like a pigpen and everybody was tired and PO'd. The guards told us maybe we'll get there tomorrow. The scenery was nice but all of the towns were badly bombed. We saw many locomotives and cars that had been shot up badly and were sitting on sidings—not a pleasant sight. Others in a roundhouse were in good shape. We saw French and Russian enforced laborers in all of the marshalling yards. They smiled and winked at us and made "V" signs with their fingers. The Germans warned us about trying to talk to them. I got into hot water by pulling the emergency brake and stopping the train. I expected to be shot on the spot—and I could have been! This incident finally ironed out okay, and though I expected to hear of it later, I never did.

September 28

After four nightmare days we arrived in Barth, Germany—our destination. We were met at the station by more guards who were accompanied by very nasty-looking police dogs. After being counted several times we began marching through Barth, a quaint little town, to our new permanent address. I don't relish the dogs.

We reached camp—a really big place—in about half an hour. We were interviewed yet again, searched, and any cans of food we had left were punched with holes. (I thought this was a very low trick; later I found out that it was standard operating practice). We were deloused and showered. An English doctor talked to us, hoping for war news. He has been here four and a half years.

We marched on to our new home. This was to be in the North Camp. Old Kreiges [veteran POWs; from Kriegsgefangener, German for prisoner of war] peered at us from behind the barbed wire, with lots of wise cracks and leg pulling. We found out later that they knew more about the war than we did.

Assigned to Block 5, Room 13, I am officially a POW. I am also split up from George. Four of us new men move in with nine Old Krieges; the "youngest" of them has been here seven months. They have a big kettle of stew for us. We all have many questions. Lights out at 11 p.m. And so I begin my Kriege life.

For security reasons, Frank Pratt did not write about how the POWs got their war information. However, in his 2007 Newsweek *interview, he recalled that the men in his barracks had a radio hidden in a panel behind a fireplace. It had been assembled from parts smuggled into the camp and the POWs were able to tune into daily BBC news broadcasts. They got the word out to the rest of the camp by writing down the essentials, then stuffing the paper into tin cans weighted with stones and tossing them over the barbed wire fences between the compounds. The POWs had "ways and means with the guards" (e.g., by offering chocolate and cigarettes as bribes), and could distract them when needed. The Germans were well aware that the POWs were getting information about the war beyond the official propaganda, but either they "never figured it out," as Frank mused in 2007, or they weren't concerned enough by that stage of the war to take the trouble to do so. The guards, presumably, were just as keen for the war to end as the POWs.*

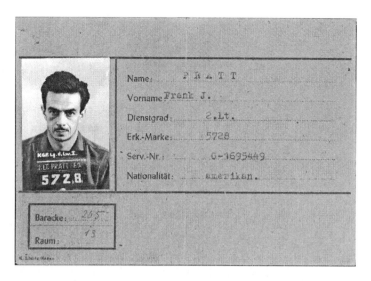

Kriege #5728. Frank Pratt recovered his mug shot and identity card from the prison camp records at Stalag Luft I in in Barth, Germany, after the German guards deserted their posts days before the end of the war. The undated newspaper clippings are from either the Mount Vernon Daily Herald *or the* Mount Vernon Argus, *both published in Skagit County, Washington.*

Lt. Frank J. Pratt Reported Missing

Lieut. Frank J. Pratt, bombardier serving with the 15th Air Force in Italy, has been reported missing, according to a telegram received by his wife from the war department. Mrs. Pratt resides in Blanchard.

The telegram, bringing word of the disappearance of the bombardier, stated that he was lost in a mission over Poland September 13. It was his 43rd mission. He had recently received the Air Medal and two oak leaf clusters.

Lieut. Pratt is a former member of Al Weidkamp's band. He attended the Western Washington College of Education at Bellingham and had been employed as manager of Standard stations in Bellingham before his induction into the service.

Prisoner of War

Lieut. Frank J. Pratt, who was reported missing in action September 13 in the European war theater, is now a prisoner of war in Germany, according to a telegram received here today by his wife. Lieut. Pratt was serving as a bombardier with the 15th Air Force.

Stalag Luft I

Stalag is a contraction of Stammlager, which derives in turn from Kriegsgefangenen-Mannschafts-Stammlager (Camp for prisoners of war). Luft is Air.

Stalag Luft I was situated on a peninsula outside of Barth, Germany, a small town on the Baltic Sea. It was opened in October 1942 as a camp for British aircrews, although Americans began arriving there shortly afterwards. By the time Frank Pratt arrived, in September 1944, the camp had been expanded several times and housed more than 6,000 men, all officers, in a series of adjacent but separate compounds. The newest of these were the three North compounds, completed in February, September and December, 1944, respectively. North I had been a former Hitler Youth camp and had a communal mess hall, running water and inside plumbing. North 2 (in which Frank Pratt was housed), North 3 and the older South compound all lacked adequate cooking, lighting, heating, washing and toilet facilities.

American and British POWs administered themselves separately but maintained a close liaison. The Americans were divided into four groups, each with a commander and staff responsible for administration, security, discipline and welfare of their group. Collectively, they operated as a Provisional Wing Headquarters, with a Senior American Officer (SAO) in overall command. At the time of Frank Pratt's arrival, the SAO was Colonel Jean R. Byerly. He was succeeded by Colonel Hubert Zemke, a USAAF Eighth Army fighter ace, upon Zemke's arrival in the camp on December 16, 1944. Among German personnel at the camp, turnover was high, with five different men serving as Kommandant in as many years. At the time of Frank Pratt's arrival, the Kommandant was Oberst [Colonel] Willibald Sherer. He was replaced in January 1945 by Oberst Warnstedt. [www.b24.net/pow/stalag1.htm]

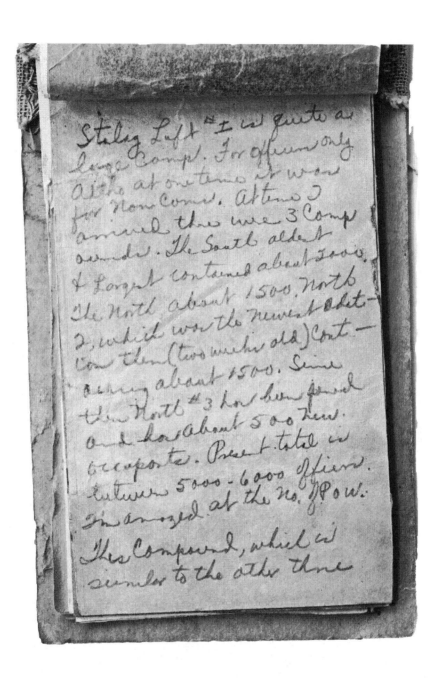

Life as a Kriege

Stalag Luft I is quite a large camp. At one time it was for non-coms, but now all the POWs here are officers. At the time I arrived there were three compounds. The South was the oldest and largest and contained about 2000 men. The North had about 1500. North #2 had been added only two weeks previously, and housed another 1500, including us. Since then, North #3 has been opened and has about 500 new occupants. So the present total is between 5000-6000 officers. I'm amazed there are so many of us.

The North #2 compound, which is similar to the other three, is square in shape and 5-6 acres in size. It is completely surrounded by a double barbed wire fence, with a "runway" between the inner and outer fences that is approximately four feet wide and filled with loosely coiled barbed wire. The fences are approximately ten feet high, with ten-inch squares formed by interwoven strands of wire. Twenty-five feet before the inner fence is a smaller fence about three feet in height. This has double strands known as the "warning wires" and anyone caught between them and the inner fence is definitely off-limits and may be shot by the tower guards.

There are towers at each corner of the compound and mid-way along each side. Looking like ranger stations, they sit about twenty-five feet high and are partially enclosed in glass. Each tower houses one guard, a telephone, two powerful searchlights, a machine gun, and plenty of ammunition. They command a very nice view of every square foot of ground in the compound.

At night the fences are well lit with flood lights, while the searchlights constantly and systematically probe the darkness. Outside the compound a roving guard on each side keeps an additional lookout, just in case. Inside the fence, after lock-up (8 p.m.), a guard with one of those nasty police dogs patrols all night. All of this makes one think twice about trying an escape.

**

Our compound is made up of eleven buildings—nine barracks and two latrines. All the barracks are of uniform size and construction, each being approximately 120 x 50 feet, with thirteen rooms and an emergency latrine for use during air raids and during lock-up, when we are not allowed outside. This latrine is not a very sanitary gadget.

Each barracks contains about 160 men. Three small end-rooms house four men each—usually the "wheels" of the barracks [i.e., higher ranking officers assigned to administrative positions]. The other ten rooms contain sixteen men each. These larger rooms have dimensions of approximately 20 x 16 feet, and are furnished with a minimum of utensils. My room, #13, has one stove with a top 18 x 24 inches in size, two medium-sized dishpans, one water bucket, and two metal water pitchers. The bucket is used for everything from cooking stew to boiling clothes. Each man has a bowl, cup, knife, fork and spoon. Extra tins, used for baking, have been hammered out of Klim cans. [Klim was a brand of powdered milk issued to POWs by the Red Cross to increase caloric intake. It was advertised in America using the slogan, "Spell it backwards!"]

The rest of the furniture consists of seven double bunks, two lockers, a table and four benches. This more than fills the room, so one double bunk has to be kept in the hallway. The bunks have wood-shaving bags laid on eight slats; after a couple of nights the bags can't be distinguished from the slats. Bed clothing is a sheet and two blankets. If we pile on extra clothing and a few empty boxes, it's possible for us to keep warm at night, providing the temperature doesn't get too low.

Each block [barracks] has a captain as commander. The C.O. of the compound is a lieutenant-commander, as is his executive officer. His adjutant is a major. The camp is run much like Army camps in the States, except that rank isn't shown as much respect. All of the compounds are under the charge of a senior Allied officer who is a full colonel. He, of course, is under the authority of a German C.O. from whom he takes orders. Apart from possible block searches, roll call, and an occasional sweeper, the Jerries leave the rest of us pretty much alone.

**

Kriege life is rather aimless. The only musts are two roll calls a day, one at 9:30 a.m., the other at 3:30 p.m. At these times we fall out on the parade grounds and form in squadrons (blocks), so we can be counted by a Jerry officer and two SMs [? sergeant majors]. The process usually takes about twenty minutes, unless the Jerries miscount. Then they get the idea that somebody is missing, and we may be standing out there for an hour or so. This isn't pleasant during cold weather. These are the only things the enemy demands of us, and otherwise we may do whatever we like. Actual pursuits are few, especially when the weather is bad and we must remain inside. Reading and just plain sack-time are the most popular ways of passing the time. The library, which contains several hundred books, is the chief source of reading material. Most of the books are pretty poor but every now and then you read a good one. Good weather allows for softball games, volleyball and football, or just plain walking around and around the lot. Night time is used up playing cards or checkers, writing or reading, or just arguing about nothing. The nights are longer than the days, and the days have been really short this past month. Daylight begins about 8.30 a.m., it's dark again by 4 p.m.

Kriege Pastimes

ARGUING: I'm convinced that no subject how complicated or trivial has not been argued at some time or other. Few people remember what was said for everyone is trying to make himself heard & consequently not much is gained.

BRIDGE: Tournaments & just so-called friendly games.

CRIB, GIN RUMMY & CHECKERS POKER & CRAPS

READING: Pretty fair library, although mostly English written books [i.e., books written by English authors].

Kriege Pastimes, continued

SACK TIME: Hour after hour!

DAY DREAMING: Along with sack time.

SCHOOL CLASSES: For a few who get in there are six-week courses in Spanish, French, Law, Home Planning, Art.

THE 'GLEE CLUB'

DANCE BANDS & PLAYS

MOVIES: I think there are two movies in camp. One features, Deanna Durbin, which I saw once, & Andy Hardy's Double Life. These are shown about every three months but get a little monotonous.

CAMP SHOWS: Are usually very good. Several songs have been written here. Among them "Law's the Sin" and "Hit the Bottle".

KNICK KNACK MAKING: Stoves, pots & pans, cups, etc. out of tin salvaged from cans.

HOME PLANNING & POST-WAR PLANS

VOLLEY BALL, MINIATURE GOLF & SOFTBALL

FOOTBALL, SOCCER & PERIMETER PACING

EATING (when there is food) is about the biggest issue in Kriegeland. After all, meals are all we really have to look forward to.

Food

The Germans, although seemingly good natured and obliging, dream up a lot of petty nuisances and otherwise get by with the bare minimum of provisions required by the [Geneva] Convention. All of our canned food was punched with a sharp tool when we first got here, so that it would have to be used quickly or else spoil. This made fish or anything with juice in it very messy. The reason for the hole-punching was to prevent the food being taken along by escapists—as if anyone who got out would care to pack a load of canned food. More recently, all the cans in our Red Cross parcels have been completely opened and their contents dumped into bowls and other cans. The Germans say this is in case of airborne invasion—we can't feed the enemy by saving food for them.

**

Red Cross Parcels are little cardboard boxes about 12" x 12" x 4". They are the delight of every Kriege. Each contains an assortment of foodstuffs and tobacco that makes POW life more bearable and a helluva lot healthier. Without them, our daily meals would be monotonous as the Jerry rations, although life sustaining, offer little variety. With the Red Cross provisions in addition to the German rations we have a healthy diet and a varied one, although the results depend on the ingenuity of the cook, as he turns his culinary dreams—and sometimes nightmares—into reality.

The Germans ration us to one parcel per man per week, except during times when a shortage occurs, and then the ration period is lengthened. To date, two weeks has been the limit between parcels, and we keep our fingers crossed during shortages for fear we may "have had it." Each little bundle of happiness weighs about ten pounds, after all, and with 8,000 men in camp receiving them this makes for a considerable tonnage each week. And from what we hear, [transport facilities] aren't abundant in these parts.

The content of the parcels are uniform, with only slight exceptions:

1 can Spam
1 can corned beef
1 can margarine (1#)
1 can jam (1/2#)
1 can pate (1#)
1 can powdered milk (1#)
1 box crackers (12)
1 box cheese (Kraft)
1 box cube sugar (1/2#)
1 box prunes (1#)
5 packages cigarettes
1-2 "D" bars (vitamized chocolate)
1 box vitamin C tabs (12)

The Red Cross organization is to be complimented on the work it does to provide us with food. Life in this place is pretty dull, but it is made much more endurable by the presence of their little 12 x 12 x 4 parcels.

The German ration consists of more perishable goods, such as spuds and bread, which we receive every day or so:

Dark bread (1/6 loaf per man per day)
Margarine
Potatoes
Sugar (3#'s per week)
Salt

German rations also occasionally include:

Cabbage
Meat (canned and fresh)
Barley
Rutabagas
Carrots
Sauerkraut

When Frank Pratt first arrived in Stalag Luft I the German food ration provided 1200-1800 calories per man per day. As 1944 drew to an end, this was progressively reduced to 800 calories. At the same time, Red Cross supplies became so low that they, too, were, cut back. Thereafter, deliveries were erratic, and for some weeks in the spring of 1945 no parcels were distributed. As later diary entries indicate, the men were continually hungry during this time. Eventually, in April 1945, Red Cross shipments were resumed and food rations continued to be sufficient thereafter.

Kriegeland Menus

FUDGE: 1/2 lb sugar, 4 tablespoons Klim & 1 teasp. Choc.

CAKE: Rolled crackers, Klim, margarine, raisins, sugar & water. Mix to thick consistency & bake. Weighty but good. (Molasses added improves the finished product.)

FRENCH FRIED POTATOES: Use oil from margarine which is melted & strained

PUDDING: Same as cake except mixture is boiled. Oatmeal may be substituted for crackers.

PRUNE WHIP: De-nutted prunes cooked. Heavy paste of Klim & sugar & water.

PRUNE JAM: Cut up dried prunes & sugar boiled down

PEA FLOUR GRAVY: Margarine or meat for base, Klim, water & browned pea flour to thicken

MASHED RUTABAGA: Sugar or molasses & light Klim mixture

STEW: The works, with Spam or corned beef

Kriegeland Menus, continued

BAKED SPAM & FRIED SPAM

CRUD SOUP: Dehydrated vegetables

MASHED POTATOES

MEAT LOAF: Corned Beef, dried bread, onion, spam & water

BACON SPAM: slice real thin & fry on real hot pan

ICE CREAM: Made from snow. Real thick & sweet Klim paste with chocolate. Mix in clean snow to desired thickness (excellent)

CHOCOLATE SPREAD: Melt down D bar, add little sugar & margarine & a little Klim

SARDINES & TOAST

CORNED BEEF & CABBAGE

SUGAR SPREAD: sugar browned and melted to syrup. Add small amount of water. Good on bread.

CHEESECAKE: Cottage cheese, prunes, rolled graham crackers, margarine. Use own judgment adding water. Mix well. Put in pan sprinkle with crackers & margarine & bake in real hot oven for 10 - 20 minutes. About 1/4 of mixture should be cracker crumbs.

CANNED SALMON & CHEESE: Mix & heat until cheese melts. Makes fair sandwich spread.

BULLION [sic] CUBE: sprinkled over buttered bread & toasted is okay!

In the Hospital

On the evening of Oct. 11, while reading *Lost Horizon* [a best-selling 1933 novel by James Hilton] and munching on a "D" bar, I had an attack of pain such as I had never encountered before and hope that I never encounter again. It came on gradually, on my right side, and felt as if someone had inserted the point of a knife in my side and was slowly continuing to push it to the hilt. I tried moving in various positions in hopes of releasing the pain, thinking it may be only a cramp. Nothing I could do would relieve it and I was beginning to double up when one of the boys noticed me.

Getting a doctor is quite a little task after lock up; but the interpreter acted quickly and a guard fetched the doctor in what I thought was record time, considering he was about three blocks away. The fellows put cold packs on my side in the meantime, which relieved the pain a little. I also did a nice job of being sick. Naturally the general opinion was that I had appendicitis and the doctor seemed to be pretty well convinced of it also. At any rate I got my first ride on a stretcher, but can't say I enjoyed it. It seemed that with every step the boys took the knife drove further in.

I was put in bed at the hospital around 10 p.m., I guess, in a ward with seven more fellows. I didn't care what happened to me at that particular moment. Three doctors came in and after a lot of dire pushing and prodding they decided I didn't have appendicitis. I wasn't unhappy about this diagnosis, because I didn't relish an operation in Kriegeland. But I was never more glad to see a needle than I was that night, especially one that was filled with morphine.

I had a pretty rough night after the dope wore off but the pain was nothing like it had been before.

The doctor informed me that the cause of my pain was a kidney stone, and they were going to try and help it along a little bit. All I had to do was lie in bed and wait for it to make its passage through me. After the first day I felt only a very slight pain and in a way I began to enjoy my new home, especially as the bed had springs.

**

There were eight patients in the ward. Also Mac and the English Major. The doctors were all English, the orderlies also—very nice but very English. All were three- to five- year POWs.

We were served meals in bed. There were characters who looked in on us through the door every few minutes.

Altogether I spent ten days in the hospital and I'm sure they will be my most enjoyable days in Kriegeland. But nothing in the way of a kidney stone came out. I've been bothered a little by it since. The doctor says I will be sent to New Brandenburg [a larger POW camp with hospital facilities, sixty miles to the south] for observation, next time men are shipped to that camp. I don't know how I feel about this. I think the pain might be caused by something that pulled loose during my parachute descent. Time will tell.

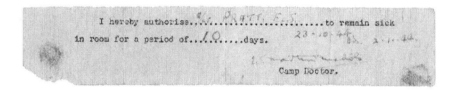

One of the compounds at Stalag Luft I, photographed with a camera smuggled to the POWs by one of the guards.

Christmas, 1944

Three months ago, when I entered the portals of this barbed institution, I was thinking silently to myself that, although possible, it wouldn't be probable that I would be here on Christmas. Today is December 25— Christmas, I believe. So I shall say, I have spent my <u>first</u> Christmas in Kriegeland. I underline "first," for in my brief visit here I have found that optimism is the thing most often exploded the loudest in these parts. God knows, I don't want to spend two Holiday seasons here, but something inside me says not to say that "I won't."

Despite the ever-present barbed wire enclosure and the multi-armed guards in the their glass-enclosed towers peering down at our every move, Christmas in Kriegeville went off rather smoothly and proved to be a welcome diversion from the everyday humdrum life. Between the Red Cross and the German efforts we were able to deck our room in keeping with the Holidays and to eat plentifully. Although the talk was light and indifferent as to the day, and a carefree spirit seemed to reign, there were times when we dropped our guard and said something that reflected what all of us were thinking about deep inside— Home. However, most of us realized that what we missed was missing us, too, and there wasn't much reason to let the "homiest" day of the year get you down. It just ain't good for the ulcers.

Getting back to what has been going on for the past few days— which is interesting, I think, for I don't believe any American home was in any more turmoil preparing for the gala occasion than was this particular room and its fourteen occupants: Naturally there were fourteen budding geniuses in the art of interior decorating, all giving their ideas on how the crepe should be hung and the tree (which was at least two feet high) should be decorated. And, naturally, when the actual work began, most of it fell on two or three. However, despite the many little disagreements here and there, the work was finished. The little Christmas tree had a green ball and a many-colored one, with the brilliance of both balls magnified by cellophane icicles (taken from cigarette packages). There were red and green streamers from the center to each corner; a green tissue curtain with red trimmings; and "Merry Christmas" in seven-inch letters, each wrapped in red and green and draped down from the ceiling. The presence of all of these things changed the room from a rather drab affair to one with a cheery atmosphere.

Snuffy, our whip-cracking cook, began planning and preparations for our feast at least two weeks beforehand. About four days before Christmas he turned out his first cake, which was a two-layer affair with a strawberry jam center and a white-and-brown icing topped off with nuts—it was really a beauty. Another single-layer cake and two pies were made later on.

The cakes still amaze me. Though they have a cement-like texture and a weighty bulk, which is unbelievable, they always turn out to be tasty morsels that are relished by all. Proof of this is the fact that only one pie remains intact at this time—and it has possibilities.

New Year's Eve, 11:00PM

In very few minutes '44 will have had it! And '45 will be bowing in for a twelve month stretch. To me, New Year's Eve is the date with the most to it. Why, I don't know. It's just one of those things. I do know I feel worse tonight about being here in Kriegeland than I did at Christmas time. However, I'm not contemplating Hari Kari [sic] or such because I am here, but believe me when I think back on past year endings I can feel just a faint touch of the old blues.

I can't remember any other New Year's Eve, at 11.30 p.m., when I would be interested in using a pencil, as I'm doing now. Kriege life does odd things for a person. Some of the boys in the block celebrated with a prune concoction they've been brewing this past week. Those who partook of the potion either became very ill or passed out, so the madhouse that reigned a few hours ago has subsided almost completely. In my case, it'll soon be four months since I partook of any intoxicating beverage. So I figure myself quite an abstainer. I think my New Year's Resolution shall be not to touch a drop until I get to the closest bar.

The Germans gave us a big break for the holiday. They opened North #3 and are leaving the lights on until 1 a.m. I wonder how they can afford it! The compound put on a talent show tonight. The fellows who attended said it was pretty good. I didn't go—hearing music and noise isn't so good for my morale.

Tonight may be the quietest New Year's Eve I have spent, but I dream of past years: a chattering mob, drunken New Years greeting's, spinning bull fiddles and a general hell raising. But, in general, the thing I miss most is that twelve o'clock kiss from Georgia [Frank's wife] that would really start the New Year out right and scratch all bad moments of the past year at the same time. Yep, those few seconds were always my biggest thrill of the year. This year I'll have to take a rain check, and just silently wish and hope that everything is fine at home and that Georgia is like always, and that she will be thinking of me as much as I am of her. I wonder what she'll be doing at ten minutes to twelve?

Well, the past year has been a pretty exciting one and probably one of my most adventurous. I owe the Gentleman with the beard many thanks for pulling me through a couple of close ones and I want him to know I appreciate it. My biggest wish for the New Year, of course, is to get home and for the whole world to get back to normal. That will be the day! But, here it is 12:00, midnight. A few strains of Auld Lang Syne can be heard, as well as jubilant Happy New Year greetings now and then. I think I'll just call it a day and hope that this time next year I'll be someplace else. But to keep in the swing of things, I gotta say, and not too loud:

Happy New Year 1945

... & Goodnight!

Three months ago, when I entered the Portals of
this borded institution, I was thinking silently to myself that, altho possible, it wouldn't be probable
I would be here on X-mas. Today is Dec 25 — X-mas
I believe. So I shall say I have spent my first
X-mas in Kresge Land. I underline first, for in
my brief visit here, I have found that Optimism
is the thing most often exploded the loudest in these
parts. God knows I don't want to spend two Holiday
seasons here, but something inside me says, not
to say that "I won't."

BOOK II

Guard tower, Stalag Luft I.

Kriege Dictionary

KRIEGE: Name given to all POW's, actually means "war" in the German Language.

"ROUND THE BEND": Men who begin to show the effects of POW life.

"OFF HIS ASS": Same as Round the Bend.

SHOT DOWN TIME: Length of time a Kriege has been down.

WHEEL: One usually of the higher ranks who holds an administrative job such as C.O., Adj., etc.

COG: One of the lesser wheels in charge of smaller jobs.

COMPOUND: One division of the camp or a stockade.

BLOCK: One barracks.

COMBINE: Room's food supply.

KRIEGELITE: Small kerosene lamp used for after lights out and or blackout.

SEARCH PARTY: Usually 20 or so Jerry soldiers & officers who search barracks for various things. Sometimes accompanied by dogs.

TRADER: A member of each block who speaks German that trades with Jerry guards.

Kriege Dictionary, continued

INTERPRETER: German talking Kriege or American speaking German.

FEARLESS FOSDICK: Plane used by flak school to practice tracking.

BUZZ BOYS: German flying cadets who train around the camp.

"HARD LUCK": A reply given to someone's misfortune.

WHEEL HOUSE: Administrative barracks.

WHIZZO: Kriege blower stove.

COOLER: Jailhouse.

FLEA HOLE HOTEL: Interrogation center at Oberusal outside of Frankfurt.

TRANSIENT CAMP: Wetzlar.

CRUD: Dehydrated vegetables.

DONKEY DICK: German sausage similar to liverwurst.

NIX GOOT: No good [from the German nicht gut].

IRON BALLS: Dried peas.

ON GUARD: Warning called out by goon guard when Jerry enters barracks.

BLOCKHEAD: Commanding officer of the block or barracks.

The Tide Turns

After a long sleepy spell, the Russian front awoke on Saturday, January 13th, and began another of its lengthy power drives. This awakening came as somewhat of a surprise to most of us, as recent failures by the Reds in East Prussia led us to believe the strength of the Crimson Tide had about spent itself. However, German observers had noted several times that great activity was taking place all along the Eastern front, and that a major push could be looked for at any moment. German news, although accurate, is usually taken with the proverbial "grain of salt", just in case—but in this case, what we had doubted became a reality, and to our joy the Red Star is proving to be far from spent.

The first reports of the new push reached us on the 14th, when we learned thirty kilometers [eighteen miles] had been gained and realized this was not just a local action. The front had put out three spearheads which were moving fast, with adequate infantry following. By January 16th, fighting had resumed in Warsaw, and on the 17th this thorn in the Russians' side had fallen to them. Needless to remark, Kriege morale soared. In the first four days of the new offensive the Russians had gained sixty miles and were nipping at the nearest port in Germany itself. It seemed dream-like that the Russkies could move so much, so fast.

The only question was, could they keep up the pace? On the 18th, Krakau was "capoot" [sic] and morale continued to rise. Numerous rumors circulated to the effect that Germany had framed all of the gains and would likewise take them all back on a big "framed" counterattack, to show her people she still was powerful—but these rumors were all exploded by authentic reports. In the meantime, Russia had branched out in all directions: northwest towards Danzig and Konigsberg, west towards Breslau, and southwest into Silesia, Germany's little Ruhr.

Today is January 24th. Every day the Germans have been

expected to stem the tide, but each day's news is of new gains with no signs of slackening yet. The suspense is terrific and the tension grows daily. Everyone realizes that this could be "it". No one wants to say this is the time [that the course of the war has changed], but deep inside they all think it is. As the latest reports stand, Red armies are on the Oder river along a forty-mile front approximately fifteen miles from Danzig, having cut eastern Prussia off at this point. Russia claims German casualties have been high: 60,000 killed and 250,000 wounded. Germany admits that this is one of the dark hours and brave hearts are needed to stop the onslaught—which will be stopped! We, too, know it must stop sometime—but when?!

New Brandenburg

In late January, 1945, Frank Pratt was sent with several other prisoners to Stalag II-A/Oflag-67 in New Brandenburg for medical observation. Sixty-five miles south of Barth, this camp offered more extensive medical facilities than those available at Stalag Luft I. As Frank writes, however, conditions in the New Brandenburg hospital were appalling. For many patients death was more likely than recovery, and had Frank not been able to trade cigarettes for food—something he seems to have been warned about in advance—he might have starved.

Frank refers to the "different nationalities" in the New Brandenburg camp. Stalag II-A was built originally to house Polish prisoners from the German offensive in September 1939. It was soon expanded to include an officers camp (Oflag II-E, later renamed Oflag-67), and to accommodate new waves of POWs in the wake of subsequent German advances. The Poles of 1939 were followed by Dutch, Belgian and French prisoners in 1940; British and Yugoslavs (mostly Serbs) after the Balkans campaign (1941); Russians after Operation Barbarossa (1942); and Italian internees after Italy's capitulation to the Allies (September 1943). From November 1944 to January 1945, during which time Frank was briefly in residence, the latest arrivals were American soldiers captured on the Western Front.

From February to April 1945, New Brandenburg became a transit stop for Allied prisoners forced to relocate on foot from more easterly camps, which the Germans had begun to evacuate ahead of the advancing Russian Army. One of these camps, to which Frank refers, was Stalag II-D, located near the Polish border city of Stettin [Szczecin]. This was eighty miles to the east of New Brandenburg—an eight-day march for its evacuated inmates.

Vernon Christensen, the surviving non-commissioned officer among Frank Pratt's ill-fated B-24 crew, was subjected to an even more grueling series of evacuation marches from Stalag Luft IV, in what is now Tychowo, Poland. Christensen was kept constantly on the move between February 1945 and the end of the war. Although he survived this ordeal, many of his fellow POWs died of starvation and exhaustion. [https://en.wikipedia.org/wiki/Camp_Fünfeichen; Jerry Whiting]

Gentlemen & Vultures

In a sugar box on a shelf in my locker, you will find a chain with my dog tags and a ring attached. I should like some kind soul to take care of same and see that they are mailed to my home address, "just in case." One never knows, during these trying times, what momentous events may take place. (How touching..) No foolin', I'd appreciate the favor – you could even send it C.O.D. However, I do hope I return in time to see all of your smiling faces before that great day (Christ! I haven't left yet). The address by the way; Box #124, Blanchard, Wash. (If a blonde answers come up anyway). Thanx – Pratt.

Pick up 4 cartons of cigs at the hosp. storeroom. I couldn't take them – hard luck.

Room – 13
Blk. – 5
North #2

Frank's note to his roommates on what they should do with his possessions if he failed to return from New Brandenburg.

January 28th

A month ago I had a little more trouble with my side, and asked the doctor about it. He immediately put me down to go as one of the next party to New Brandenburg, where there are specialists to deal with such matters. Then [yesterday] I was informed I should be ready to leave for New Brandenburg in five minutes. I had all but forgotten about the deal, so the hurried call was somewhat of a surprise to me. But I was ready and reported to the [Stalag Luft I] hospital, where I stayed all night. I was thoroughly searched and allowed to keep only one package of cigarettes with me. I had brought seven cartons, most of which were left behind.

Monday morning: Up at 5:30 a.m. with seven others. A one and a half mile walk to the station at Barth. A blizzard the night before had covered the road with snow to a depth of two feet, so the going was difficult and cold. But it felt good to be free of the barbed wire for a while, and we arrived at the station in time to make the train. A big crowd of people stared at us, holding their noses, as we stood around.

We rode for half an hour and changed trains. The second train was crowded, and we rode in the baggage car. After another half-hour we made it to Stralsund [fifteen miles southeast of Barth]. No trains would be going to New Brandenburg for six hours. We stood around for a while. The guards made telephone calls. In the meantime we saw some 10-12 year-olds from the Hitler Youth Movement. A lot of people are on the move, evacuating from Silesia. We marched down to German marine barracks [in Stralsund], where we played cards and fooled around until it was time to catch the train. We reached New Brandenburg about 6:30 p.m., then walked uphill for two hours in snow to the hospital. No one who was sick could have made it. What a rat trap this hospital is. Dirty. Bedbugs. Lack of food. I wanted to go back to [the Barth] camp immediately. But the different nationalities here are interesting.

February 5

Just about this time three years ago, the furthest thing from my mind was that I would be [spending my third wedding anniversary] in a place like this. I have thought of that day and its events hundreds of times. How I'd like to do it over again. "Whoops, my dear!" Happy Anniversary, Sweetie, wherever you are. Next year maybe we can be together.

February 8

Two years since Uncle Sam sent me that special delivery [i.e., U.SA.A.F. call-up papers] and wakened me from a nice sleep. What an eventful two years!

I'm still in New Brandenburg. Results of tests show I do not have a stone. I don't know what it could be, but I still have pain now and then on my right side. I'm not saying anything because I don't wish to be detained here any longer than necessary. Besides, the doctors here have little in the way of medicine to offer. The bed bugs have really given me a working over. I'm supposed to go back to Barth any day now. It's not pleasant there, but better than this place.

The reason for our delay is no doubt due to the war. The news we get here is not too reliable, but it is quite certain the Russians are not more than a hundred miles from here. Reports say New Brandenburg is full of evacuees. Several hundred sergeants arrived yesterday from a camp in Stettin. They're a pretty sorry lot. I hope we don't have to walk [i.e., evacuate camp].

February 11

The Sabbath, which is the same as any other day. The past four days seem to have slipped by rather fast. Lots of rumors are flying around about the three Allied powers meeting somewhere [Yalta, where U.S. President Franklin Roosevelt, British Prime Minister Winston Churchill, and Soviet Premier Joseph Stalin met to discuss Europe's post-war reorganization]. I'm anxious to learn of their discussions. Lots of other people are anxious also.

Thursday night was an exciting one, as I saw my first night air raid. Flak looks wicked at night. I saw one ship explode. One of the gunners was brought in our ward last night with two broken legs. The biggest scare for us came from flares dropped over the camp and New Brandenburg. I thought for sure we would be bombed, but the flares just indicate a turning point for the planes. It's really a weird feeling to hear the drone of hundreds of ships in the dark of the night. Stettin and Berlin, both about seventy miles from here, were both hit by the RAF.

The Russian drive has slowed down, but reports say the western front is moving again. It looks as if the tide has definitely turned now. Most everyone figures the war will last only a few more months. The new arrival—the English tail gunner—says three months at the most. I hope he is right. He is a plucky fellow, thirty-six years old. He's pretty badly broken and bruised, and has just been informed that his left leg is badly shattered below knee.

The American next door died Friday night. He was an infantry man from the western front and had quite a struggle with life for two days.

I may leave for Barth tomorrow—I hope!

February 18

Back in Barth again. Arrived Thursday [February 15]. The events of the past week were interesting and a little morbid. On Tuesday night, in New Brandenburg, we were informed that we would leave for Barth on Wednesday. I was plenty happy to be leaving that filthy hole [the New Brandenburg camp]. We walked to the station again but I was glad to be out in the fresh air and away from barbed wire. It seemed like freedom of sorts. New Brandenburg was a mess of evacuees. For several days before we left, a steady stream of wagons, carts, etc. could be seen coming from the east. Upon arriving in New Brandenburg, people discarded their vehicles and transferred themselves and their personal belongings to trains. What a mess. They were mostly old men and women and young kids. The trains were already jammed full, so people sat between the coaches, despite the weather being plenty cold.

It took us seven hours to go the forty miles to Stralsund. We arrived there at 9:30 p.m., right in the middle of an air raid. I got separated from the rest of our group—five POWs and two guards—in the turmoil of the station in the dark, so that I actually had to look for them. It would have been easy to escape, but without knowledge of the train lines this idea seemed rather ridiculous.

Having missed our train connection at Stralsund, we were marched through town to spend the night at the marine barracks. The streets were darker'n hell! On arrival we were put in a basement air raid shelter with some nice looking women. Being so close to something feminine gave me a strange feeling—after all, it has been a long time. From the shelter we were moved into solitary confinement, but the cells were very clean, with a table and three blankets for a bed. I was tired and slept well despite the cold and hardness of table.

We were wakened early, before daylight, and marched back to the station. Even this early in the day, the place was jammed with evacuees. Evidently they had been there all night. Babies were crying and the station was generally a helluva sight. On a siding, there was a train of sixty to seventy freight cars, full of people and soldiers. Apparently there was no straw in the cars, and people were relieving themselves out of the doorways. What a price people must pay for mistakes [i.e., of their leaders/governments].

As POWs, we were not molested much, except by words. Some butcher-type called us swine and killers of women and children. I can think more than I can write about that type of bully at present.

Before leaving Stralsund, we picked up a B-17 navigator from the camp in Stettin. One of his legs was gone. He said the Russians were about seven miles from Stettin.

Our train arrived at Barth about 10 a.m. I was glad to be back. Although the camp is a hole, it's still better than the hole I just returned from. The peace and quiet in Barth seems good. But the food shortage here is critical now, the coal shortage is bad, and the weather is cool.

February 19

One hundred and fifty wounded enlisted POWs arrived in camp today. They were a sad looking lot. As usual, they carried many rumors from

Stargart [the camp at Stettin]. They claimed they were completely unguarded for three days, and had been waiting for "Joe" [i.e., the Russians]. Then their guards returned and they were all evacuated.

February 21

The weather was the biggest topic of the day. It was a beautiful spring day and the sun felt mighty fine—enough to make me homesick. I could practically smell grass and leaves burning.

News is pretty much at a standstill. No lights tonight, and the food situation is critical. Oh well, what the hell.

March 2

I've been rather lax about writing the past few days. One reason is that we have had no lights for the past week. The second reason is that most of my daytime hours have been taken up playing poker.

To date the Germans haven't given much explanation for the lack of lights in the barracks. They want us to think they screwed up their calculations, I guess, but the Russians are evidently raising a little havoc with the power system.

It doesn't help any to be without lights. Although the days are light until about six o'clock now, the night hours drag and about the only thing to do is to hit the sack early. Ten o'clock finds everything quiet and sometimes it happens even earlier. Personally, I crawl in to bed about 9 p.m. Of course, going to bed early makes for getting up early, and 7 a.m. finds a lot of the boys up and around. So it makes a longer day. A guy can't win!

The poker game started about ten days ago on an I.O.U. basis. After a player lost $50 he was out and the game carried on without him. It's in its finishing stage now, and only three of us are still playing. I'm about $50 ahead and have been trying hard to get back down to even so I can quit. The game doesn't hold much interest when there's no real money in it. But it has helped to pass time.

Our food situation stays about the same—not too good. We have been getting one Red Cross parcel per four men the past couple weeks, and although this helps it doesn't go far. We were down to only cabbage soup a few days back, but the Germans finally came through with potatoes so we're a little better off. Our main meal at night now consists of a big bunch of mashed potatoes and gravy made of pea soup powder. It tastes damn good despite the fact that there is no salt in it.

Being hungry is strange. I imagine most of it is psychological, but there is still a lot of it that "isn't". The funny thing is that everybody's thoughts seem to be of something to eat, and we punish ourselves by sitting around in the dark and talking about choice dishes we used to like, and what we'd pay to be able to eat some of those now. To me it becomes almost unbearable at times, and I was never much of an eater. I can't imagine what hunger must do to a gourmet!

Circumstances like these show that money really doesn't mean everything. I don't believe there's a person here with less than $1,000 coming to him, yet we can't buy what we want and it definitely doesn't fill our stomachs. Little 20-cent "D" bars are selling for $15 at present. I hope this lesson sticks with me, and that I will remember in future years that food is the greatest comfort there is.

The war situation has begun to pick up again. The Americans are about five miles from the Rhine at present and the Russians are about the same distance from the Baltic. With the continued cold but clear weather the Air Force is pounding away and the future looks a little brighter. I've been thinking the past month that maybe we will see the end of the war in June or July.

Yesterday's German communiqué included some corres-pondent's [highly imaginative] version of events: How the Germans hoped the white nations would join with them and fight off the Russian hordes. How there will be revolutions in the U.S. and England. This was a "defeated" speech if I ever heard one, and very much different from those of a couple years back. My only comment in response to the Germans' so-called strife is "Hard luck!"

About 150 more sergeants arrived from the east a few days ago—evacuees. They had marched about 200 miles. I know a couple of them. They had heard nothing of the other six members of our crew.

March 10

A year ago today my semi-natural way of living came to an end. Since then, in my estimation, things have been pretty much of a mess. In a way, it's been a rather educational year—but I would just as soon have lived the old life. I wonder where I'll be a year from today?

Last night we had lights for the first time in about a month. I must say it seemed quite unusual. The food situation isn't getting any better, and my stomach is really objecting to the "lay-off." Our main meals consist of potatoes one night, rutabagas the next. I never knew either one could be so delicious. Rumors have it that the Red Cross parcels have arrived, but so far we haven't seen any of them.

Another rumor that's gaining momentum, and for which a lot of fellows are preparing, is the evacuation of the camp. I'm not much in favor of it, but who am I to object? If we're not moved soon it's going to be too late, as the Allies seem to be opening up. The Russians are about eighty miles from here now, and the Americans crossed the Rhine Wednesday. We should all be feeling great jubilation but I guess pessimism and hunger don't put one in the best of spirits.

Wehrmacht [regular army] guards have replaced the Luftwaffe in camp. If Germany is as hard up for manpower as these new men suggest, then it is high time she threw in the towel. None of them appear to be less than fifty years old, and the majority are all around sixty-five. Some look even older. They deserve pity more than respect.

Radio loudspeakers have been installed in the barracks, so now we have music and news [in German but translated by German-speaking Krieges] for three or four hours a day. It does help. The weather is trying hard to be spring-like, but late snowfalls keep interrupting.

March 12

The Americans seem to be doing all right to date. The bridgehead along the Rhine is now twelve miles long and two miles wide. Patton [General George S. Patton, Commander of the U.S. Third Army] is one mile from Koblenz. This really is what everyone has been hoping for, but enthusiasm is sadly lacking and very little is ever said of the good position the Allies now command. I expect if there were a few more full stomachs we Krieges would be a lot happier. The food situation is a bad one, with no sign of help close by. I keep telling myself it could be worse. However, I can't ever remember being as hungry as I have been this past week.

Rutabagas have become a rare delicacy and black bread has begun to take on the aspect of cake. I suppose someday I'll be able to look back on this as a joke. I hope I shall never forget what a comfort food is and that when I do get access to the stuff again, I won't bitch about any of it, no matter how untasty it may be.

A year ago today (Sunday) we finally got to Morrison Field. Six months ago tonight I was taking my last drink of Italian gin. Little did I realize it was going to be so long between drinks. Hard luck. A 35-cent fruit cake, shipped from the States about six months ago, sold for $42 today. A "D" bar was raffled off. Eighty packs of cigarettes were in the raffle also.

A Dream Menu, March 12

Breakfast

Oatmeal - thick cream

Waffles - maple syrup

Fried ham & bologna

Fried potatoes

Toast & coffee

Lunch

Rice tomato soup - Crab Louie

Hot beef sandwich - (*beaucoup* gravy)

French fries - (Catsup!)

Milk

Apple pie & coffee

Dinner

Several drinks of good Bourbon

Crab cocktail - salad

Huge T-bone - (Catsup!)

French fries

Coffee & Banana cream pie

March 13

Today marks six months in this hole. A year ago I was eager to start out on my big adventure. And what an adventure it has been.

The news is about the same. Kustrin has fallen and the American bridgehead has been enlarged. The rumor about Red Cross parcels turned out to be false. My left shoulder is plenty sore tonight, as is everyone else's, as we all had typhoid booster shots today!

March 17

Sure and it's the Irishmen's day today. Nothing much green around here. Nothing much of anything, in fact.

The typhoid shots really raised hell with us. I was pretty sick for a day. Had a tooth fixed yesterday. American dentist, not bad.

The war fronts seem to be sitting down again for a reorganization period. Probably preparing for another spring offensive!

The food situation is about the same. A sergeant in North #1 was broken [beaten?] for stealing a rutabaga. Finally located Blodgett, one of the navigators on our ship. Rather amusing the way we met on the fence, especially when Canin [3rd navigator on the same mission] came up.

March 18

My prediction of the war fronts quieting down was a little wrong yesterday. Patch [General Alexander M. Patch, Commander of the U.S. Seventh Army] and Patton both seem to be moving rapidly on the western front, and the Russkies drove twelve miles on the eastern front around Ratibor [Raciborz, Poland] and are on the outskirts of Stettin, about seventy-five miles from here. Things may happen yet!

Two fellows were shot today for being outside after the air raid siren sounded. One died tonight. It seems a pretty rotten trick but fits with the Germans' idea of keeping us under control.

March 21

The first day of spring, I believe. The sun was out today, and lovely, but the wind was mighty strong and cold. I wonder how it was at home? Last year on this day I was pretty close to the equator. Oh well, that's the way it goes. Wonder where I'll be this time next year—not in Germany, I hope!

The news has been good today. The Americans linked up close to Mainz and now occupy all of the west of the Rhine except for 40 miles. The bridgehead is twenty-five miles long now. The Russians destroyed the German bridgehead at Stettin. That's all good, especially the latter, as it's close to here. I hope the Russkies drive across to Rostock and cut us off here. Wishful thinking, I guess, but it's thrilling to think it possible that we could be freed in a week. Oh well, time will tell!

Two fellows were caught stealing food from a storeroom. They will be dealt with pretty harshly, probably. It's too bad stuff like that has to happen, but an empty stomach doesn't have much conscience, believe me!

There's a rumor of mail being in. I sure hope there's something for me. We've had another big issue of spuds. These should last about two weeks. They're not good alone and without salt, but they're filling.

I attended a camp show today and it wasn't too bad. The glee club and cabarets were very good, but I couldn't quite see the band.

I feel like breaking my non-predictory mood tonight, so I'll say May 22. Gee, that's only two months away! Well, it could be!

March 22

The news is quite sensational again today. Patton and Patch are really going to work on upper Rhine. Ludwigshafen has been entered and the bridgehead is twenty-eight miles long at Remagen. Air forces are having a field day destroying troops and materials. Improving morale and optimistic talk is quite noticeable in camp this evening. The Russians have thirteen armies at Stettin and vicinity, which looks good to my way of thinking. However I'm not too optimistic yet. I guess I'm afraid to be.

March 23

Ludwigshafen has been taken. New Krieges shot down five days ago were not even interrogated. The biggest rumor/question of the day: "How many men can walk five miles?" Are we going to move?

March 24

A great news day, and morale is really high. Patton crossed the Rhine and drove ten miles east. Montgomery [Field Marshall Bernard L. Montgomery, at that time the British commander of the 21st Army Group, comprising the British Second Army and Canadian First Army] crossed up north and paratroopers made a landing twenty miles east of this crossing. Earlier in the day our optimism was darkened by the news that we would be moving out of here soon. But the belief is still pretty general that we won't evacuate, and even the arch-pessimists were stirred by today's events. I still remain quite calm.

Today I spent my first money in Kriegeland, in the form of a check. I paid the fantastic sum of $3.00 a pack for cigarettes. Two and half cartons cost me $75.00. I realize it's quite extravagant, but cigarettes are mighty scarce and there's not much probability of them becoming more plentiful. I guess I can afford it, and besides, they help me stave off the hunger pangs that come all too frequently of late. If I ever get out of here that check will always be a reminder of when times were tough!

March 26

The beautiful weather these past few days has been remarkable. It's really like what we get at home, and it has spurred all kinds of activity around the compound, from playing ball to washing clothes and planting a garden. This has added to the biggest and best war news yet. Patton has raced across the Rhine, as has Montgomery. Paratroopers dropped twenty miles ahead have linked up with the armies, and things in general are really moving—fast! Optimism is really high and even the firmest

Frank's hand-written $75 check for cigarettes. The recipient, Sam Walker, tried multiple times to cash it after he returned home, but without success. Eventually he mailed it back to Frank in Blanchard.

pessimists believe this thing can be over in April. How I hope they are right. As for myself, I seem to be coming out of my indifferent attitude and think that this might be it.

Rumors of moving have died down a little. We got an issue of horsemeat today and it really tastes fine and is a little more filling than the usual old spuds.

March 27

The offensive rolls on and the news contains signs that bigger things are to come, and fast. Patton is in Frankfurt and the Remagen bridgehead has broken out in two places. The Russkies are only 45 miles from Vienna. All this, along with the arrival of Red Cross food parcels, has made the day a red letter one in Kriegeland. Red Cross parcels were issued today, one to four men, and will be issued again tomorrow. What a feeling to have food (of a nature) again. It is rumored that ten carloads are due in within the week.

The room went on a two-combine [?double food ration] schedule today. Quite a mess but maybe it will work out alright.

Another rumor says that we will have twenty-four men to the

room soon. We have nineteen now and I used to think fourteen was crowded! New arrivals say civilians have changed their ways of thinking about airmen and are a little more friendly. This is quite a change, if so.

Despite all the good news today I'm in a blue mood tonight. No mail again, and I had really planned on getting some today. I hope it has only been mislaid somewhere. One's imagination can play funny tricks. What the hell. Hard luck.

Frank with five of his roommates: (back row from left) Al Braca, Harold Hammond, Jim Pearson; (bottom row from left) Julian Spiller, Bruce Knoblock, Frank Pratt.

March 29

I'm just about convinced I should get on the bandwagon of optimism. Things really seem to be happening on the western front. Patton is going wild and Montgomery is moving fast. I still think I shouldn't let myself believe this is it, but with a full stomach once again it is mighty hard to be pessimistic and I'll concede that the end won't be too long now.

We have really eaten well today, and I have just finished a snack. What a feeling. Rumors say that we have a month's supply of Red Cross parcels on hand. That's fine! We may be moved out any day, but most of us think that the recent turn of events will cancel that.

I've been making plans to improve the Blanchard property when things have quieted down. I hope I don't run into any snags with my relations.

Mail call yesterday proved of no value to me.

Frank's wife Georgia had been notified by telegram that he was missing after the September 13 mission, but she did not receive confirmation until December that he had survived and was a POW. Even if she had written to him immediately afterwards, incoming mail at Stalag Luft I spent months in transit partly due to censorship delays. Most POWs received their first mail only after they had been in the camp for half a year or more. Towards the end of the war mail deliveries were even slower due to transportation difficulties. Sending mail out was also problematic as letter and card forms, like other forms of rations, were generally in short supply. [www.b24.net/pow/stalag1]

April 1

Happy Easter and April Fools Day, all at once. A year ago I went to church in Africa. Today, although there were church services, I skipped them. I'm a bad boy. I guess the most noteworthy thing of the day has been the food situation. Not since Christmas has there been such plenty, and how we have eaten! I'm uncomfortable now and I still have a huge piece of cake to eat—I don't think I'll make it. It's really incredible how circumstances can change in a week. Last Sunday we were starving to death, and today we're rolling in it with plenty more in sight. Along with the good news, it has made us all really high. What a feeling!

All fronts have been moving the past few days and many people think we will see an end to this thing in two weeks. But a German broadcast today stated that Germany's occupied territories would resort to guerilla warfare. That's not good.

Got a new boy in the room today. He was shot down this week and is from Italy. He had a lot of disturbing news.

The weather hasn't been too nice of late. Easter bonnets in the Fatherland, if there are any, will probably get wet.

I wonder what my wife is doing today?! I hope I hear soon, else I'll begin to think something might be wrong. Oh well. I know that today, for once, I have been contented, and despite the barbed wire I can say it has been a Happy Easter.

Vultures' Happy Easter Dinner

Spam fried with cheese
Mashed potatoes & gravy
Tuna fish loaf
Dried peas (iron balls)
Raisin cereal pudding with Klim sauce & coffee
Coffee & cake

What a meal! Quantity and quality.

Chef: J. Meatball Snype

April 3

A year ago we landed at our destination in Africa!

Good news continues to come in, plenty of food and even coal are at hand, and one of the most amazing things was a BBC broadcast that just ended and really panned the Germans. I still can't believe it, but I heard it with my own ears. I think the war has definitely turned and even I expect it to end soon. Betting is down to "How many hours before the war is over." The usual reply is, "Sorry, I don't have a second hand on my watch." Tonight, I think my May 22nd prediction is a little pessimistic. I hope so!!

Max Schmeling [celebrated German boxing champion and

Luftwaffe pilot, well known to Americans for his bouts with Joe Louis in 1936 and 1938] visited camp today and caused quite a stir. Dressed in civilian clothes, he's a nice looking fellow and gave out autographs.

April 6

Big day for me today because I received my first contact from home. Surprisingly, it was in the form of a parcel, and a very lovely one at that. It is unusual to get a parcel before a letter but that's the way things seem to happen in my life. It was sure a wonderful feeling to receive it, and of course I was the envy of the room for a few minutes. Life here takes on a new light when a guy hears from home, I mean…!

Meanwhile, the war rolls on. Nothing sensational but slow, good gains. The Americans are 137 miles from Bonn and about 200 from us, and the Canadians are only about thirty miles from Bremen. Rumors of the Russians starting a big artillery barrage from Stettin to Sudetenland tops things off. If this is true, then the Reds are planning on moving again, and that should just about finish it! They are only seventy miles from us now. We still might move, but I really think we won't, as there really isn't any place better for the Germans to take us than here at Barth.

April 8

Sunday again and pretty bad weather. League softball games are being played tonight, however. Our barracks is right on the playing field and we get a good view from our window.

I used my new razor and blade [sent from home] this morning, and gee, what a swell shave! A little mentholatum afterward. Boy, what a lovely feeling. I reckon that razor will be my most prized possession while I'm here. The cheese is mighty fine also!

A German news broadcast just put the Allies at Schweinfurt and on the outskirts of Hanover. Shouldn't be long now! Sure gives me a thrill to think this thing is coming to a focus. Something will no doubt happen to mar my optimism—it usually does—but the way things have been going another two weeks should bring the Russkies and Americans together. Meanwhile, the Germans have turned from arrogant Supermen into very mild mannered mice. They even apologized for miscounting us at roll call yesterday and causing us to remain in formation five minutes longer. What a change! They're really trying to get on the bandwagon.

April 12

Tonight I end this little book [Book II] and it is on a cheery note.

The allies are a little south of Magdeburg tonight, or seventy miles from Berlin. This represents a sixty-four-mile advance in twenty-four hours. The map on our wall is green like hell, and about the only white left is about a 100-mile corridor. Our half of Germany has gone by the boards. Optimism is really high and everyone feels it will be just a matter of days. News has all been good the past few days. Food is plentiful and the weather beautiful. This is not a bad place to be under these conditions.

My career as [a softball] umpire began again yesterday, and I umpired again today. The season opened in style with the colonel throwing the first ball. The spectators are difficult at times, but I enjoy being part of it.

Air activity is great around here tonight, which gives one a funny feeling. We expect the Russian front to open up any day. There's much talk of going home, which also seems funny—hard to imagine! I hope it won't be long. And how I hope! As I've often said, time will tell!

Room #13, Barth, Germany

Bruce D. Knoblock	Sturgeon Bay, Wisconsin
Julian E. Spillers	Hope, Arkansas
William N. Roberts	Dallas, Texas
George T. Regan	Yazoo City, Mississippi
William I. Whitney	Norwich, New Jersey
Ralph H. Pearson	Jamestown, New York
Charles H. Lundsberg	Greenville, Michigan
Harold E. Hammond	Florence, Alabama
William J. Young	Ukiah, California
William C. Lordon	Philadelphia, Pennsylvania
Alfred G. Braca	Staten Island, New York
F.K. Osborn	Tampa, Florida
Ralph N. Winslow	Taft, California
James D. Pearson	Banquete, Texas
Glenn A. Weiss	Cooper, South Dakota
Anthony Santamanes	Molden, Massachusetts
Thomas A. Davis	Oneida, Massachusetts
Curtis E. Orr	Houston, Texas
Dan A. Theokas	Lowell, Massachusetts
Parke Wright III	Tampa, Florida
Everett Robson	Fort Smith, Arkansas

'Inside the Barbs' spaghetti sauce

1 large Bermuda onion
3 lbs good spaghetti
1/2 pt olive oil
6 oz. can tomato paste
8 oz. can peeled seeded tomatoes or (peeled fresh tomatoes)
pinch of thyme or (rosemary)
4 tablespoons sugar
1 lb. chopped pork
1/2 lb. chopped beef
Parmeggiano cheese
salt & pepper

Fry onion (finely chopped) in oil, browning nicely. Add paste & tomatoes, thyme, salt & pepper. Simmer for about 1 hr. then add pork & beef & cook for minimum of 2 hrs. Garlic may be immersed for a minute or so for flavor. Pour sauce over spaghetti. Serves 6.

HOT SAUCE: Sear 2 hot peppers over open flame. Chop finely and add at time of tomato paste.

MUSHROOM SAUCE: 1 lb. chopped, fancy mushrooms browned in deep butter, to be added to sauce an hour after meat.

MEAT BALLS: (instead of Meat Sauce & Spaghetti). Cut proportion of meat in sauce to 1/2. Meat balls are two parts pork to one part beef. Mold balls firmly with garlic smeared hands & drop into boiling sauce for 10-12 minutes. Bread crumbs added to meat when taken out.

DELUXE SAUCE: Add sliced hard boiled eggs to sauce just before pouring over strained spaghetti which has been sprinkled with cheese.

'Inside the Barbs' was an internal camp newsletter.

Miscellaneous notes

Charcoal for broiling outside or for picnic use. No smoke & plenty heat.

Dry cement sprinkled in flagstone cracks keeps grass down. Moisture from ground hardens it.

In response to a Picadilly Commando's high prices: "I came to save your —, not to buy it."

"I don't mind if I do, ol' boy - I don't mind if I do."

Remember to write Jim for some fresh pineapple, Curt for pecans & Red for peanuts.

Use chicken wire for flagstone reinforcement (or sidewalks).

Margarine or butter makes good base oil for candle light in an emergency.

Hot cakes fried & spread with butter, sprinkled liberally with sugar plus a bit of cinnamon & stacked & placed in a warm oven for a while reported to be okay.

French toast, after being fried on one side & turned over, may have the center cut out (about 1" diameter) and an egg broken in removed place.

Egg fries while second side of toast is frying - sounds okay!

Right at this moment I have an awful craving for a chocolate malted milk with two raw eggs beat up with it & a little nutmeg.

Miscellaneous notes, continued

Peanut butter mixed with plain butter makes better spread than straight peanut butter. A little syrup or sweetening added to spread improves the taste.

Boiled Klim (mixed with little water) makes good glue.

Tin can nailed on stick makes good clothes plunger in an emergency.

German margarine & thick Klim paste make good creamy mixture.

Write Whitney for maple sugar about March 1st.

Osborn can contact some good cigars in Tampa.

Boil de-nutted prunes until soft .Mix rich Klim goo. Put prunes in pie crust made of cracker crumbs, marg. & Klim. Pour goo over the top - really tasty pie!

Ground peanut brittle added to whip cream is a tasty dish - they say.

BOOK III

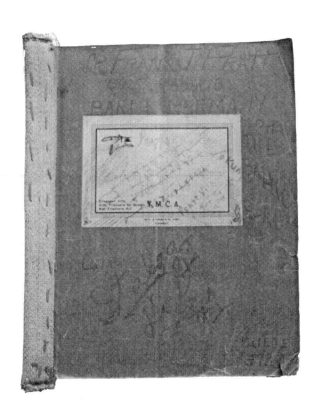

Lieut. Frank J. Pratt, of Blanchard, a prisoner of the Germans since September 13, has been awarded the Distinguished Flying Cross for extraordinary achievement in aerial combat in the North African and Mediterranean theaters of operation, according to official word received by the flyer's family. The flyer was specifically cited for a mission over Austria last June 16.

Frank Pratt's Distinguished Flying Cross (below left) and Air Medal.

Waiting to be Surprised

April 13

1900 hours. President Roosevelt's death was a great shock to everyone in Kriegeland. There was much comment as to what effect it would have on the Germans and on the war effort. Naturally, it is too early to tell but the Germans, surprisingly, treated his passing with noticeable respect. How they will use it later on remains to be seen.

War news has been especially terrific today. At present the Allies [Americans, British and Canadians] have pushed to Wittenberg, approximately sixty miles from Berlin, less than a hundred from the Russian lines, and 110 miles from here. That is a gain of sixty miles in the last twenty-four hours. It is almost unbelievable that such an advance could be made—in fact, it has had a dazing effect on most of us. To think that we are only a matter of days, possibly, from being freed from this hole seems like a dream. Yet the Germans have admitted to all of the gains, so the news is quite sure to be accurate. On the eastern front, the Russians seem to be preparing to launch another offensive. There has been great air activity in the region last night and today, and the Germans reported "Luftwaffe against Russian offensive preparation" this afternoon. If the Russkies open up and the Allies keep moving as they have been doing, the next few days around here may prove to be exciting indeed! The topic of moving came up again yesterday when the new Jerry Kommandant [Oberst Warnstedt] announced that if the Russkies broke out of their Stettin bridgehead and started this way, we would move west. The only catch is that since he made that announcement, the Allies have moved at such a rate as to drown almost any thoughts of evacuating from here. Only today, POWs have been moving in from districts south of here, so once again most of us think it is rather unlikely that we will evacuate. But one never knows what's going to happen nowadays.

Received my second present today—six cartons of Camels, very fine. I must commend my wife for being on the ball. Of course, I really appreciate things like that, especially around these parts. I still haven't had any letters which is quite amazing to me, as well as unusual, because letters as a rule precede parcels of any kind. I sure hope everything is all right at home.

By the way, today marks the seventh month since the day I was shot down! Seven wasted months. I wonder, will it be eight? Tonight I say it won't be, but time will tell.

Weather today—sultry with showers.

April 14

1845 hours. The past twenty-four hours have been marked by large Allied gains. The Elbe River appears to be completely occupied by the Americans and British. Whether or not they have a bridgehead across at any point is not known. A security blackout covers most of their actions. South of here, Patton has bypassed Leipzig to the south and is reportedly nearing Dresden. He is supposedly sixty miles from Berlin at this point and about ninety from the Russkies. The Ruhr pocket has been diminished considerably. Here in Barth, the Allies are still about 100 miles from us. However, rumors during the day suggest this distance may be considerably shorter. Of course, it remains to be seen how true this is. The activity of German soldiers around the outside of the camp has been somewhat of a forecast of probable things to come. Trenches were dug several months ago all around the camp and about 100 yards from the outside wire. These are always manned during air raids, in case of possible paratroop invasion. Today, rehearsals for something else were going on, and little guessing is needed to figure out what it might be. Those machine guns are pretty thick populated out there, I mean, and it is just a trifle nerve-wracking when they're pointed in this direction. To my way of thinking, somebody's liable to get hurt before we get out of here. I hope this doesn't happen, but the Jerries seem to be trying to make the best of what for them is an impossible situation.

Air activity is increasing around here daily. Junker 88s seem to have moved in to the local airport and are operating steadily. Last night the RAF put on a nice display about forty miles southeast of here.

Numerous flares were dropped, which caused considerable concern to everyone in the barracks. Tension is pretty high, for we know at this stage that anything might happen.

Beautiful weather today. Red and I had a bad time umpiring a game. Some guys are pretty poor sports. This being Saturday, and the time of year that the summer resorts begin to open up, I've been doing a lot of thinking about Al [Weidkamp, Pratt's bandleader at home] and the band, etc. Maybe Al's in the army! It's sure been a long time since I heard anything about anybody—seven months! I wonder what everybody's drinking now. For some reason or other, this kind of weather brings back the pleasant thought of rum and coke to me. I'm sure gonna be ready to go on a good one [a bender] if I ever get out of this joint. The strange part, though, is that I don't have any special desire to drink. I guess this type of life just isn't conducive to drinking. After all, getting drunk (as if it were possible) in a six-acre field wouldn't be very exciting.

Debts so far in Kriegeland

Check to Sam Walker	$75.00
Kriege book	5.00 COD
Kriege cartoons	3.00 COD
POW wings	1.25 COD
German wings	1.25 COD
Pictures	COD
2 Red Cross parcels	COD
Plaque	5.00 COD
Book	10.00 COD
Picture	2.50 COD
Cartoon book	2.00 COD

April 15

2000 hours. All armor on the western front is moving today. No sensational advances, but still nothing to be sneezed at. Leipzig and Chemnitz are being attacked. The Allies are only about seventy miles from Russkies. In the north, the Canadians are about sixteen miles from the North Sea. The biggest news, still not completely confirmed, has been the moving of the Russian front. There has been great air activity around here these past twenty-four hours.

I'm not much interested in anything tonight. I've been in bed all day and have been feeling lousy—flu I guess. It started off with a bang about 2 a.m. this morning. The doctor tells me to stay in the sack for two more days.

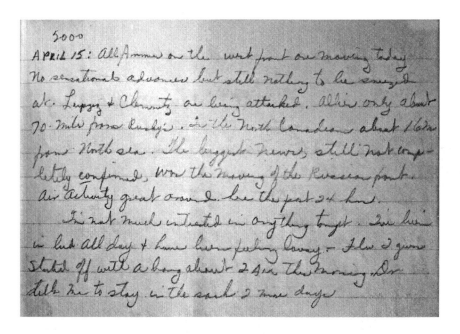

April 16

Feel much better today, although I'm still a little weak in the knees. I seem to have had a touch of the same thing so many others have had the past week. The doctors say they believe it is caused by the German bread, which has been pretty moldy and improperly prepared of late. Personally, I think a lot of it, and my case at least, is caused by overeating and too-rich food concoctions, after such a poor diet previously. I can well imagine what would happen if we were to be turned loose suddenly at home and allowed to eat everything we craved! It bears out the rumor that we will be kept on strict diet for thirty days after returning to the States.

War news hasn't been too sensational today, although I imagine we are getting rather hard to please (i.e. unless there is a gain of thirty to forty miles anymore, we think things are going slow). The Russians, and this is pretty well confirmed, have started from Stettin to Kustrin. If this is true, we should see plenty in a few days, depending, of course, on whether they drive north or south. They are about eighty miles southeast of us, the Allies about a hundred miles southwest. That ain't too far away when I stop to think of it!

We had an air raid this afternoon and the Jerries really took to their fox holes, surrounding the camp and armed to the teeth with bazookas and machineguns. It's not an easy feeling to think that Russian tanks might push over yon hillock at any moment and start spitting lead in our general direction. Nor does it soothe the nerves to realize that the air field, about two miles distant and operating as it is now, is an ideal strafing target for our P-51s. Everyone hopes that the Allies know we are here, believe me! However, there is not a helluva lot we can do about it if they don't!

Vienna fell yesterday! I remember some rather hectic times over that city and its vicinity, and I am glad to hear it is out of commission.

Beautiful weather today.

April 18

1900 hours. The past two days, although not of the exciting, sensational type, have proved interesting in that it appears, to me anyhow, that the last and the toughest of the battles in the war is beginning. It is certain that the Russkies have opened up all along the eastern front, and going by the losses announced by OKW [Wehrmacht High Command] to date, the fight promises to be a bloody one. The Reds supposedly lost 246 tanks yesterday. To do this amount of damage, the Jerries surely must have large forces protecting their front. This is suggested also by the fact that Russian advances haven't been too great, only ten to fourteen miles. On the western front, the Americans seem to be straightening their lines on the Elbe and regrouping for the final blow. Stubborn German resistance has slowed any large gains. Indentations have been straightened out in the line for a gain of fifteen miles or more, but the front as a whole seems to be pausing for a breather. Magdeburg, fifty miles southwest of Berlin, is under attack and Patton is close to Dresden (seven miles).

Air activity is still the biggest thing around here. Mostly Junker 88s with an occasional JP or FW [Junkers or Focker-Wulf fighters, based at the nearby Barth military airfield]. Their traffic pattern seems to be directly over this camp and for a while, at night, it was a little disturbing to the sleep, but I've grown quite accustomed to their droning as of late and sleep like a child (how touching!). There are rumors of artillery fire rumblings from the west—I haven't heard any yet. No lights the past three nights and water only part of the time. Daylight lasts until 9 p.m. so not having lights isn't much of a bother. The Jerries blame the power shortages on the airfield, which supposedly needs the juice. Rumor says that one division of Jerry soldiers is now occupying the flak school [south of the camp, where German soldiers were trained to operate the 88 mm guns used to bring down Allied aircraft]. The Germans order that our shutters must stay closed from 2100 to 2300. No teasing the dog.

The weather has been very fine lately and sunbathing is getting more popular. Our pool room pallor is slowly disappearing. Softball is in full swing. An All Star game yesterday was very good, 1 to 1.

April 20

1200 hours. A big artillery barrage, not too far away, began about 1 a.m. this morning. At 6 a.m. the barracks were really shaking. There was much debate as to where it was taking place. Some believe it to be

German counter attacks. I'm not sure. If it was artillery, it couldn't be more than forty miles away. The Russians broke through yesterday and are now twenty miles from Berlin. The British are eighteen miles from Hamburg. Patton is in Leipzig and Hodges [General Courtney Hodges, commander of the U.S. First Army] in Magdeburg. Things are really shaping up. A two-hour air raid just finished. We're having lots of them now. Goebbels [Nazi Propaganda Minister Joseph Goebbels] says, "The war is drawing to a close." I'm inclined to believe him. The Ruhr pocket is finished.

1800 hours. The Russians are about fifteen miles from Berlin, and driving towards Chemnitz and Dresden. News broadcasts are jammed pretty bad, making it hard to interpret. It looks like we'll have no more lights for the duration. One year ago I arrived in Italy. Raining hard this evening.

April 21

1500 hours. The Russians gained forty miles yesterday and put two bridgeheads over the Oder River at Stettin (which was the reason for artillery barrage). The Russkies are now only eighteen miles from Hodges, with a spearhead northeast of Berlin fifteen miles from the capital. No reports yet from the western front, but any gains to speak of would mean a link up. Kriege morale and optimism has hit a high mark, and well it should.

The Russian breakthrough occurred south of Berlin and went to the Elbe, ten miles southwest of Berlin.

A sergeant, Domms(?), from Everett looked me up today. He used to drive trucks for Lipman Timber and is a good friend of Ed Gee. He's married to a girl named Graves from Sedro Woolley, who is some relation to Graves Poultry farm. He used to come to our dances.

Artillery fire, frequently, in the east.

Weather not too nice. Rather cold and April-ish.

**

April 22

1500 hours. The noose seems to be closing around Berlin. Reports are not too accurate, but the Allies are believed to be fighting in the outer defense circles in the East. There's street fighting in Dessau and Bremen. The British have crossed the Elbe and are on the outskirts of Hamburg. Reports have it the Russkies have been allotted everything east of Berlin, the Allies everything west, and the British the north and northwest. It looks like we in Barth will have to start cheering for the British. Our location is really at the far end of everything. We will no doubt be the last people out of this mess. I guess I'd just as soon wait a few weeks longer, rather than walk out, as the fate of some of the other liberated POWs hasn't been too good.

Stuttgart was cleared yesterday.

April 23

1900 hours. Berlin is now encircled to the extent of 270 degrees. Distances in the partial circle vary from six to ten miles from the center of the city. The British have not crossed the Elbe in the north toward Hamburg, as reported. Hodges and the Russkies are about eighteen miles apart. News has been slight today and no gains of any nature have been made. It is the general opinion that either the Allies are regrouping a little, or else opposition is getting much stiffer. This has been the quietest day for news since the big drive began just a month ago. Kriege opinion and prophecies are still of a mixed nature. Some believe the war will finish before the end of the month, others forecast from the 15th of May to the first of June. Very few think it will last past June. Bets in the room have been screwy. Knobly is doing Lordon's next three KP's if Lordon will do his for the duration [i.e., however long the war lasts after that]. Whitney bet three "D" bars and a quart of scotch that we won't be here the 1st of May. It truly is a tough situation to try to figure out which way to bet. It could be over soon and yet it could also last for a long time. I still think my forecast of May 22, made just a month ago, will be pretty close to right.

Artillery rumblings are still noticeable during the day. Last night, flashes could be seen to the east and southeast of here. What they were hasn't been confirmed. They seemed a little like northern lights [aurora borealis] to me. Green flares dropped close to camp were a mystery.

Air activity at the local airport has died down. Whether they've lost their place or moved on is not known.

Rumor just came in that the Russkies and Americans have linked up. I hope it's true. And Bologna fell yesterday. One of my first targets [the Bologna railway marshalling yards, May 19, 1944].

Weather chilly and upset today, ninety percent overcast.

Canadian Red Cross parcel issue is different and, I believe, slightly better than the American version. Real butter and lots of jam, plus more meat.

[When I get home I need to] look up the records "Sidewalks of New York" (Duke Ellington), "Take the A Train", "I'm Beginning to See the Light", and "In Everyone's Life a Little Rain Must Fall" (Ink Spots and Ella Fitzgerald).

April 25

Berlin is now about half gone and is reportedly undergoing one of the greatest bombardments ever known. Artillery, rockets and bombing have reduced the once-great city to complete chaos. News of other sectors has been good the past twenty-four hours. In the south, the French are really moving. Friedrichshafen has fallen (I had two trips over there) [July 20 and August 3, 1944, on which the targets were the Zeppelin factory and the Manzell aircraft plant, respectively], and Regensburg is not far away. Patton is moving on Prague, while it's pretty certain that Hodges and the Russkies have linked up. In the north, Dempsey [General Miles Dempsey, commander of the British Second Army] is under a security blackout again and nobody seems to know much about him, except that he is in the vicinity of Hamburg. The Russkies are attacking at Stettin but don't seem to be gaining much ground.

The German news is rather spasmodic. Of late, we have been receiving only one broadcast a day sometimes. Reports have it that Jerry communications are in mighty bad shape. That can well be imagined, for when I look at the map, there's only a minor part of Germany that isn't already occupied. We seem to be the forgotten men up this way, as all activity is taking place in central and southern section. We hear often of POWs being released in other sections and naturally we are a little envious. I guess a few weeks longer won't make much difference after all the time we've put in here.

Lots of attention is being given to the San Francisco peace conference that begins today, but the war could be over before it ends, and Berlin will still be kapoot [sic].

The United Nations Conference on International Organization, also known as the San Francisco Conference, was held in that city from April 25 to June 26, 1945. It was attended by delegates from fifty countries, with leading roles taken by the foreign ministers of four major Allied powers—i.e., the U.S., Great Britain., Soviet Union, and China—to establish the United Nations, including the General Assembly and Security Council.

Everybody here is pretty much in a nervous state about the whole thing, although we all try to be calm and poised. As someone put it this morning, "it's like waiting to be surprised at a surprise party." Every little thing that happens is a bid for the end of the war. Rumors are now rampant, of course, and every burst of gunfire we hear, whether it be Germans practicing or not, is either the Russkies or the British coming up yon hill. The colonel of the camp caused a near panic a couple evenings back when he called an assembly to announce the mere fact that Hitler was in Berlin directing its defense. Everything was dropped and a mad, shouting, stampeding crowd of Krieges gathered around the [news?] blackboard. This proves what state of mind most of us are in. However, we all know that one of these days [the announcement of the end of the war] won't be a false alarm. I kind of dread the din that will ensue when that day comes, for I am still, like always, not a believer in such a show of enthusiasm and joy—although inside I'll probably be the happiest guy in the camp.

April 27

1400 hours. Here I lie on a blanket, on a tired patch of grass, trying to absorb some of Germany's sun. There have been nicer days than this one, with not so much haze and the wind not so strong, but I have a bench set up in front of me serving as a nice wind break, which makes for a warm spot—and I might say, the ideal way to fight a war. There is much activity around the camp today. From where I'm lying, I can see two volleyball games, a softball game, two Krieges having their hair cut, two more heating water with "whizzes," about fifty guys playing catch, and a hundred or more just milling around outside. Three or four more are doing just as I am—which, as usual, isn't much in terms of activity. From a distance I can hear a trumpet murdering "Sweet Sue," and just now a JU-88 soared pretty low over the camp. (The German engines sure sound ragged). There's the usual yelling and continual chatter going on—this accompanies Krieges wherever they are. They make enough noise at the intra-barracks softball games to sound like Madison Square Garden. These softball games are damn good, but like everything else they become boring after a while. I just noticed down by block #4 that a boxing match is going on, and a little farther on Mac is instructing his golf class in driving. Mac was one of the first fellows I met at San Angelo [Army Air Force Base, one of the four West Texas Bombadier Quadrangle schools], and he slept in the bunk beneath mine during my stay there. (You sure meet people in funny places). Yep, these nice days make for much activity around Kriegeland. Despite the fact that we all hate this place and long to be back home, there will probably be times when we wish we could be back here living such a carefree, lazy life. The lifestyle is about all that can be said for this joint, although conditions are rather cramped—due to the barbed wire entanglement that surrounds us and constantly reminds us that we are POWs.

The past week has been the first one during my stay here that we have not been short of something in the way of food, lights, salt, etc. The Jerries seem to be outdoing themselves to keep us supplied. Over the past few days we have been issued about 600 pounds of potatoes. Previously we had to live on skimpy rations.

The guards bend over backwards to be of assistance, which I no doubt would do if I were in their position. But, all in all, things are quite enjoyable—compared to a few months back.

The carefree, lazy life, Room 13.

Rumors, as usual, hold the spotlight. During the past few days, when real news has been scarce, the rumors have been out of this world. All of them have been possible but not probable. The prize one yesterday was that Jerry guards in the towers would be replaced by American sergeants at 2030 hours. No! It didn't happen.

Short as it was, the news of the last twenty-four hours is full of promise. The Russians pushed about twenty miles west-northwest of Stettin and are now about fifty miles from us. That is good news and brings the end for us a lot closer. The British and Canadians, thought to be about ninety miles southwest of us, are still blacked out and may be a lot closer. We know for certain something is going on close by, as heavy guns can be heard most any time of the day or night, and at times they really shake the barracks. Since yesterday noon we've had eight air raids. Three of these occurred between eight and twelve in the morning. Evidently it's the RAF giving ground support. The worst battle of all is going on about 150 miles south of here, in Berlin. Its intensity and size cannot even be half imagined. The Russkies supposedly have the city half cleared now. I believe its fall will mark the fall of Germany. I hope it is soon, because I do want to get home before fall.

I've been daydreaming a lot of late, wondering about home and thinking about what I'd like to do if I get back. I'm pretty puzzled about not hearing from Georgia. I know she's heard from me, or at least about me from the Red Cross, or I wouldn't have received my packages, but having no letters from her puzzles me. [German censorship of incoming mail may have delayed letters more than parcels.] I keep telling myself everything is all right, but still I can't help thinking. A lot can happen in eight months. I keep wondering whether she still thinks about me as she did when we parted. Nothing would hurt more than to find out a change had come about. Still, being a widow isn't much fun either, and I guess a gal can't be blamed too much for whatever she does. I'm confident, though, that nothing would change Georgia much, and anything she would do that would meet with my disapproval would be done unintentionally, or during one of those blue moods when nothing seems right. At any rate, I should like to know what my better half is doing. Maybe one of these days I'll hear and my mind will be more at ease.

April 29

1000 hours. Things really started coming to a focus late yesterday afternoon and on into the night. After comparative quietness on the news for a couple days, the air and ground began to shiver and shake about 8:30 p.m. last evening. It was from big guns that were not too distant, and the Kriege poured out of the barracks to get a better listen. The firing was coming from the southeast. After lockup, the firing was sporadic but it was definitely not as far away as that of the past ten days. Everyone was much concerned and talked in raised voices, proving that something unusual and exciting was going on. The 10 p.m. broadcast really made for great excitement, and bedlam reigned for several minutes after the interpreter had given the translation of news. The Russkies and Americans hooked up north of Berlin and are driving straight for the peninsula [the Darss-Zingst Peninsula, north of Barth, on which Stalag Luft I was situated]. They are about fifty miles away and seem to be pushing pretty hard. Naturally, the guns we heard and are still hearing must be connected in some way with that push, and believe me, optimism has risen to new levels. The wild talk that went on until well past midnight last night was good for the morale. Yet it was also rather inane and silly for supposedly grown men. I like to see enthusiasm shown, but I don't believe in displays of the sort some people put on. It doesn't ring true to me. At any rate, the British also broke loose and drew thirty miles northwest of Hamburg to almost reach the Danish peninsula. Bremen has fallen. All that is left of 1939 Germany could be put in a mighty small space. How they lost is remarkable.

Two-thirds of Berlin is gone. I think our day of freedom here is rapidly approaching. The biggest rumor of the day is that Himmler [Heinrich Himmler, senior Nazi official and SS Reichsfuhrer] has his headquarters in the camp and Barth.

1600 hours. An air raid is in progress at present. It broke up our softball game. Boy, am I stiff!

Things are really happening. The two o'clock broadcast was really hot. My old temporary home at New Brandenburg has been taken and the Russkies are at Ankalin [Anklam]. All in all, this front, moving

WAITING TO BE SURPRISED

this way, is only forty-eight miles away. Guns are getting closer, it seems, and their rumblings more pronounced. FW's & ME's have flocked to the airfield in the past twenty-four hours—about sixty have arrived. Things are really beginning to take place, and any hour we expect big things to happen.

The pay-off is the surrendering of Himmler to the two powers [i.e., the U.S. and Britain], but not to Russia. Things were really happening this morning at two o'clock, when the war was considered over. The United States was celebrating until President Truman told the people the war was still going. At any rate, the Germans have been given until Tuesday to make up their minds. What happens then? It's a cinch this damn thing is coming to a close. What a roar people in the States must have let forth when they heard. I must ask my wife what she was doing and what she thought while all this news was going on.

April 30

1500 hours. Things are really in turmoil today. At 9:45 a.m. we were given orders to dig trenches. We've dug and are still digging. The camp looks like all hell has broken loose. The Russians are about forty miles away and coming this way. All afternoon, demolition has been going on at the flak school and, evidently, the airport. Some of the explosions have been terrific.

We have just been informed that by tomorrow only forty Germans will be left in this camp. Fifteen hundred Americans are scheduled to leave here for Wismar, sixty miles southwest of here. One hundred and fifty Russians are going with them, taking supplies. Who is going isn't known. The commandant of the camp couldn't be found this afternoon. Planes are coming from the east all of the time. Himmler is definitely about four miles from here, at Schwerin.

Rumor has it that Hitler and Goering are dead and that Mussolini was executed this morning.

Things are happening in Barth.

**

Rumor has it that Hitler & Goering ne dead &
that Mussolini was executed thur Arm.
Things are Happening in Both

Himmler had arrived in Schwerin on April 28, together with his staff and military bodyguards. The week prior, he had been in Hohenlychen, sixty miles north of Berlin, attempting to negotiate peace terms with the Allies, via the Swedish diplomat, Count Folke Bernadotte. Without informing Hitler, Himmler asked Bernadotte to convey to British Prime Minister Winston Churchill and U.S. President Harry Truman the proposal that Germany surrender to the Western Allies, while continuing to fight the Russians. The proposal was rejected, and when Hitler learned of it, on April 28, he dismissed Himmler from all offices and ordered his arrest. With the fall of Berlin imminent, Himmler relocated to Schwerin to be close to Admiral Karl Dönitz, head of the German Navy and Hitler's chosen successor. Dönitz had established a headquarters in Plön, forty miles north of Hamburg.

As Head of State after Hitler's death, Dönitz did not arrest Himmler, but he made clear his distrust and advised that Himmler surrender to the Allies and take responsibility for all SS atrocities. Himmler and two companions fled in the guise of NCO military policemen, but they were captured near Bremervörde, Germany, by three liberated Russian POWs on May 21 and handed over to British authorities. During a medical inspection two days later, Himmler committed suicide by biting into a cyanide capsule.

Like Himmler, Luftwaffe chief Hermann Goering was declared a traitor to the Reich in the last days of the war, after sending a telegram to Hitler on April 22 requesting permission to assume control of the Reich in the event of the Führer's proposed suicide. Initially kept under house arrest, Goering made his way to American lines and was taken into custody on May 6. In the Nuremberg trials of 1945-46, he was convicted of war crimes and crimes against humanity, and was sentenced to death by hanging. He committed suicide by ingesting a cyanide capsule on October 15, 1946, the night before his scheduled execution.

Adolf Hitler committed suicide by gunshot in his bunker in Berlin on April 30, 1945.

Deposed Italian dictator Benito Mussolini was executed by Italian Partisans in the northern Italian town of Giulino di Mezzegra on April 28, 1945. He and his mistress, Claretta Petacci, had been captured the previous day. Both Mussolini and Petacci were shot, after which their bodies were hung upside down in the town square.

April 30, continued.

1800. Demolition of installations is still taking place and the flak school has "had it". The explosions started with single blasts, about one every five minutes. Before long they were going off five to ten at a time, which really had things rockin'. At present, small arms ammunition is going off by the thousands. The south compound has really been taking a beating as it can't be more than 200 yards from the fireworks. Most of their windows have been broken and the hospital roof caved in. Great billows of black smoke have been rising from the direction of Stralsund [fifteen miles east], so evidently the same thing is taking place there. Explosions can be heard from all over and the popular belief is that the whole peninsula is being devastated.

There is a rumor that Colonel Zemke will take over the camp [i.e., from the Germans] tonight or tomorrow. He says no POWs will move from here.

Our trenches are finished and my back is plenty stiff. After all, it's the first work I've done for some time and we did it almost entirely with Klim cans and boards. I hope we never have use for these new additions, but just in case we do, they look pretty good. We have a trap door through the floor for fast access.

We also have orders to fill all available receptacles with water, Klim cans and all. The Germans will probably destroy the generators. We have a maximum of four days left here. The wash room is off limits—the basins are to be filled with water.

The Gestapo have moved from camp.

Things I want to do if I ever get home again!

1. Stay pretty close to home and away from all kinds of crowded conditions.

2. A couple quiet picnics (weather permitting). Just two of us, with plenty potato salad and wieners.

3. Fix up Blanchard [Frank's property in Blanchard, Washington State] quite a bit.

4. Indulge in some good food & often.

5. Try out some Kriege recipes.

6. Sit down in a secluded spot with a quart of whiskey and get drunk all by myself (selfish fellow me). I used to do it and get a lot of stuff figured out. Maybe I can do it again.

7. Raid a well-stocked ice-box about midnight.

8. Have a beach party or something with lots of beer & wieners & mustard.

9. Fried bologna & waffles.

10. Barbeque some nice chops & steaks on that Blanchard outside fireplace.

11. If weather permitting, maybe go camping for a couple days.

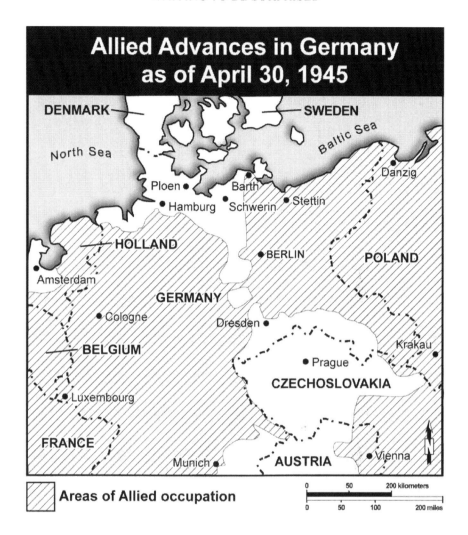

Allied Advances in Germany as of April 30, 1945

DENMARK

SWEDEN

North Sea

Baltic Sea

Danzig

Ploen ● ● Barth ● Stettin

● Hamburg ● Schwerin

HOLLAND

●BERLIN

POLAND

● Amsterdam

GERMANY

● Cologne

Dresden ●

BELGIUM

Krakau ●

● Prague

CZECHOSLOVAKIA

● Luxembourg

FRANCE

Munich ●

AUSTRIA

● Vienna

Areas of Allied occupation

0   50   200 kilometers

0   50   100   200 miles

It's Finally Over!

May 1

1300. This will go down as a memorable day in the life of everyone here. I know I'll have a memory for May 1st, as today was the first big step in ending this mess-up for us. Things came to a focus fast once they started. I was wakened this morning about 4:30 a.m. by much activity and noise in the barracks, including a portable phonograph blaring away with "G.I. Jive." Outside, Kriege were running around like mad. Two fellows from Room #13 who were up came in and broke the news to the rest of us. It seems that at midnight last night all lights were turned off. During this period of darkness, all remaining German guards left their posts and the camp, and Colonel Zemke took over the command. By one o'clock, our own sergeant guards had taken over in the town and the camp was in American hands. Today, we are an American camp in Germany, and although restricted in the camp, we might be considered free men.

The meaning of all this hasn't quite hit me, I believe, for I don't seem to feel any great excitement. It's kind of hard to fathom the fact that there aren't Germans in the town. Maybe I'll see the light soon.

On the other hand, a lot of the Kriege are walking around red-eyed from an all-night session with the coffee pot. I slept like an infant through all the excitement.

2200. Things have quieted down a little this evening. However, the BBC news that Stralsund was taken this afternoon may put some of the eager boys on "tank watch" again tonight. We received news this afternoon that the four kilometer deal [i.e., Russians four kilometers or two and a half miles away] was fake. But that Stralsund is only fifteen miles away caused much talk. Rumors have been thick today. Farm tractors were taken for tanks, wind socks for white flags, grass fires for smoke screens—and a lot of the explosions today were Jerry kids living in the flak school who had found some German hand grenades.

The biggest thrill of the evening! Listening to the radio and broadcasts from the States. It gives a guy a mighty funny feeling inside to know it's coming from there. This being halfway "free" ain't so bad. I wonder what being 100 percent free will feel like. The hit parade is on now. Kay Kyser [American band leader of the 1930s and '40s] just finished. Gotta listen to some music for a while. Life looks much better tonight.

2225 hours. The alarm was given to fall out into the trenches. The trap door was thrown open and we made it in nothing flat. When we got out we could hear the south compound guys screaming at the top of their voices. The Russians are here! The next three compounds took up the cheering and, in a moment, 8000 Kriege were really cheering. The Russians were an advance guard that left immediately.

We just had gotten back in the barracks and were listening to the hit parade when the announcer cut in with "German radio has just announced the death of Hitler." There was one big cheer and then everyone was quiet, as if perhaps they really didn't know what they were cheering about. The world's Number One trouble maker has taken the count [i.e., lost the match].

The coffee pot is being put on by way of celebration. Talk is plenty wild and noisy in these parts at present.

May 2

1530. The Russkies have arrived and we're moving on foot to Rostock, forty miles away. After all the debate about evacuating, it's finally come. We're leaving at six and everything is in a hubbub of packing the bare necessities. Good luck.

May 3

1800. Still in Barth but free to roam the peninsula. What a twenty-four hours these last have been! The Russians are rough characters and no foolin'! The ones who ordered us to march were terrors—a drunken plundering bunch—but they have moved on now, west to Rostock. Events since three o'clock yesterday afternoon: a Russian colonel told Colonel Zemke to tear down fences and let us out. He [the Russian] was PO'd that we had to stay behind barbed wire after we had been freed. Colonel Zemke tried arguing. The drunken Russian pulled a gun and the fences came down. Then 8,000 Krieges went mad. Fences were broken down, towers ripped apart, spotlights broken, and mob rule took over. The flak school (what was left of it) was raided. Thousands of brand new German uniforms of all descriptions were found there, and woolly winter helmets, steel helmets, officer's hats, and snazzy flying boots, were carried back by the dozens. Every Kriege wore German garb of some kind. German bicycles, hundreds of them, were brought back as well. All hell had broken loose.

A mile up the peninsula, warehouses stocked to the ceilings with supplies were looted. There was GI clothing of all descriptions and sizes that was supposed to have been issued to us and wasn't. Light bulbs were broken by the hundreds, crockery was smashed, and great general destruction reigned. In Barth, which was crowded with drunk Russians and drunk Americans, the German people were scared beyond help. Russian tanks were wrecking and looting jewelry stores, battering down civilian doors, and shooting up the town. Tanks were careening down the narrow streets at breakneck speed. One ran into the corner of a building and tore off the corner. The Russkies cheered. GI trucks [lend-lease equipment provided to the Russians] rolled through by the hundreds on the way to Rostock. Women were crying and moaning, young girls were being chased, American prisoners were being harassed by Russians. Germans begged the POWs to stay in the town overnight to protect them from the wild Russians, who care for nothing. The beautiful big church was used for Russian barracks. Chicken feathers and tin cans were strewn everywhere inside. Russians took horses and carriages from civilians and gave them to the POWs, who drove them back to camp. They did the same with autos and motorcycles. That the sight was indescribable is about all that can be said.

On the bay shore, a half mile from here, lay three women, two children and a baby in a carriage, all shot through the temple. Suicide, it is said. A horrible sight and a representation of war and its horror.

Nets in the bay were lifted and fish galore were carried into camp. Geese, live chickens and rabbits were traded for cigarettes and chocolate, or just taken. The stew pot here has been going all day today.

Refugees [German civilians] tried to get into camp for protection from the terror of the Russian presence.

Kriege, after being locked up for months, are quite spellbound by all of this excitement. Those who can speak foreign languages are making great progress with liquor and women. Many headed for the barracks, two miles away, of a thousand or so forced labor girls, most of them Polish. [These girls were probably assigned to the Barth Heinkel aircraft factory.] Some mighty bleary-eyed boys came back into camp today.

Today was a different story. Martial law was declared in Barth, and the town is off limits. We are limited to the territory north of the South Compound. Colonel Zemke stood up to the Russian colonel last night and that's why we didn't have to walk. In a twenty-minute address, the colonel told us of what had happened and the hell he had gone through over the past day.

Colonel Zemke, as the ranking Allied officer in Stalag Luft I, had been informed on April 28 by Kommandant Oberst Warnstedt that the Russians were less than twenty-five miles away, and that the camp was to be evacuated within twenty-four hours and relocated to Hamburg. No transportation was available, so the 9000 POWs would have to march the 150 miles west. Zemke persuaded Warnstedt that it would be better for him and his fellow Germans to depart quietly before the Russians arrived, and for Zemke to take charge of the camp. When the Russians arrived, Allied MPs were occupying the guard towers and the Stars and Stripes was flying in place of the Nazi swastika atop the camp flagpole. As the Russians tore down the barbed wire fences, Zemke was informed by their commander that American Air Forces were not allowed to fly over Russian-occupied territory, so the Stalag Luft I POWs would have to be moved to Odessa. Zemke, who spoke some Russian as well as fluent German, sent his British counterpart, RAF Group Captain C.T. Weir, to ask Field Marshal Bernard Montgomery to negotiate with the Russians (specifically Marshal Rokossovsky, commander of the White Russian Army Group which now occupied Berlin and the Baltic region) to allow the U.S. Eighth Air Force to airlift the POWs out of Barth. [www.merkki.com/zemkehubert.htm]

The colonel has not been in contact with American forces yet, but he's trying. The Russian terrorists have moved on and the surrounding country is being occupied by a slightly saner bunch. We have been given permission to roam the peninsula but the town is off limits because five Kriege were supposedly killed in town last night. Those Kriege who took off for American lines are to be charged with desertion. (I don't think the charge can be made to stick). All bicycles are to be confiscated for MP use.

All during the day gunfire could be heard in Barth and another smaller town three miles away. We could well imagine what was going on.

All during the holocaust [of the past two days] I think I've kept my sense pretty well. I'm opposed to destruction of property; although I answered a secret request within my mind to smash up about five big earthenware pitchers at the storehouse. This took the tension off and I was kind of ashamed afterwards. I haven't been too much enthused, I guess. I've seen a lot, and I'll never forget it, but it hasn't driven me either to drink or to chasing women. Today I enjoyed myself as much as I have for years by taking a walk through the woods. They are beautiful, and gosh, it's an awful good feeling to be free again and not have a damn guard looking down your neck. I climbed up in a couple of the towers and took a look. Not a week ago it would have been TS [tough shit] to even touch a warning wire. It is a queer feeling, when I stop and think about it, to be practically free.

Food is so plentiful now, it's pathetic. We have no lights but what the hell.

The crowning news came about 4 p.m. this afternoon, and that is that we'll definitely fly out. We're waiting for further details, but rumor has it that it will be within the next forty-eight hours. Jesus, I can't believe it. I'm gonna make some more fudge.

The breaking news came about of the ? & were waiting for further details & that is that well definitly fly out. Rumor has it, it will within the next 48 hrs. Jesus I can't believe it. I'm gonna make some more fudge.

Local Airmen Take Part In Barth Revolt

Five Skagit county families are vitally interested in a press story released this week which tells how 9,000 imprisoned Allied airmen seized Stalag Luft 1 near Barth, Pomerania, and went "back to war" on May day in time to be in at the final phase of the European conflict.

It is known that Captain Carman Rhoades, Lt. Jimmy Hutchison, Lt. Harold (Bud) Cannon, Lt. Frank J. Pratt and Lt. Frank Hayden were among the men who were imprisoned at Stalag Luft I. However, no word has yet been received of their welfare.

The men who waited long for such an opportunity seized control of their own prison camp and conquered nearly 200 square miles of Germany when their Nazi guards prepared to pull out as the Russian army approached Barth. It was a long rehearsed operation, in which the prisoners of war stormed and took the guard tower and radio station, established picket and skirmish lines and sent scouts in all directions.

There was little opposition. The airmen disarmed the nearby Germans and swiftly captured 50 vehicles, thousands of weapons and 3,000 gallons of fuel, as well as bagging 2,000 prisoners. Five nearby prisoner of war camps and one concentration camp were liberated and the Barth air base was taken with 14 aircraft in flying condition and 16 others only slightly damaged. By evening, contact was established with Allied forces on the Baltic front.

May 4

1800, Russian Saving Time. Things have quieted down a little today and Krieges, confined to certain areas, have been amusing themselves in various lazy ways. I believe eating has taken up the most time. Rationing is over and whenever a person feels like eating, he goes at it. This is quite a difference from times past. I know there has been ten pounds of fudge made in our room alone in the past day.

I enjoyed myself thoroughly today. Jim and I took off about 10 a.m. with spam, spuds, cheese, coffee and bread and had a picnic out in the woods. It was really lovely. The weather was fine, the scenery is beautiful around the Baltics, and the food was delightful. (Remind me to roast some spam.) We lay around and gabbed till about 4 p.m. this afternoon. That old feeling of freedom really is a good one.

The Russkies have quieted down considerably, although some of their deeds, which I shan't mention here, weren't the best. A new Russian commander issued orders today. They contained few words, and were mostly to stay in our own backyards. I think Krieges are beginning to understand.

The best news of the day is the statement by Colonel Zemke that the airport, after being closed, is ready for incoming and outgoing traffic. Officers sent to the American lines made contact, and one of them has been taken to England to make plans for our evacuation. An OC-3 (Russian) is due to land here presently with AM GOT [occupation government] personnel to supervise our leaving. All in all, it seems to bear out the rumor that we'd be out of here in 48 hours. I do hope so, you know! The saddest thing of the day was a funeral for three French forced laborers. They were among 200 people found at the airport, shackled together in a pit. They had been left that way by our good German friends, and had not been fed for days. Twenty-five of them aren't expected to live. Things like that leave me with no pity for what's happening to the Heinies now. I suppose a lot of innocent people are suffering, but a larger percentage of them aren't innocent, so to hell with 'em. Let them be wiped off the map, as is being done.

I've turned the slit trenches into a sand lot for myself and am having lots of fun working in the dirt with a big trowel that I looted. The fellows say I'm balmy and off my a---; but I'm happy! Nothin' the matter with me, doc!

2000. News has just come in that all German forces in NW Germany, Denmark, Heligoland and the Frisian Islands will lay down their arms at 0800 in the morning.

May 5

1400, RST. Organization is coming slowly back to camp. The Russian colonel and aides were inspecting today. Russian troops marched through on their way to the point. Another concentration camp was located in that vicinity [a satellite of the Ravensbrück camp for women, situated near the Barth military airfield]. Martial law is still in force, and although conditions have improved it still isn't advisable to go out of bounds. Russian MPs are on guard around camp and those boys ain't to be fooled with. A lot of fellows are still taking off for Allied lines at Rostock. This is against orders, and to avoid MPs they have been going by row boat or raft across a small lake to a neck of land that is not under guard. From here they proceed to the south-west. It is a dangerous adventure and I don't believe it shows very good judgment.

If they make it, I suppose they will have lots of amazing experiences to talk about. Personally, I would just as soon wait out the short time we have left here in comparative safety. Reports are that Rostock is overrun by every nationality of POW and that it will take two to four weeks for them to be cleared through there.

Our latest poop on moving is that we will be moved out of here by "Wednesday". If that turns out to be true, I'll be happy about the whole thing. For the first time I'm perfectly content to stay here for a while.

Yesterday, the Russkies asked us if we needed anything. One of the things requested was fresh meat. Today, we have a huge chunk of fresh beef on the table.

The Russian commandant ordered us to wear mourning bands for President Roosevelt. We are wearing them.

1800. Just returned from assembly. Colonel Wilson had some pretty good news on evacuating us by air. Contact is made and preparations have definitely begun for us to be flown out, and within the next day or so.

This afternoon a major, a captain and two GIs drove up in a jeep. They were from the Rostock-Lubeck area [west of Barth] and were really given a welcome. They were the first free Americans we had seen for some time. Three Russian generals and marshals were here at the same time. One of the marshals [Rokossovsky?] was Russia's Number One soldier and distinguished himself at Stalingrad and Stettin. He was a squatty-built fellow with a row of ribbons from shoulder to shoulder.

Tomorrow, Montgomery is due here. Why all this rank should visit, I don't know. News correspondents were taking pictures and names today, and they said that by tomorrow our folks would know of our safety.

May 6

2100. Russian daylight time sure makes the days long. It's broad daylight at ten o'clock now.

Things are still a little messed up around these parts. Krieges are trying to get out and MPs are trying to make 'em stay. It seems that the boys, including myself, are getting a little restless and want to go home, so they've been taking off in droves for the American lines, thirty-five to forty miles west of here. The colonel has given orders for everybody to remain in camp, threatening those who choose to leave with DD [dishonorable discharge]. To back up his order, he has placed hundreds of MPs on guard around camp. Some of them are armed. It has cut down the moving out a little, but several hundred have still gotten get out through various methods—row boat, raft, etc.

I was all set to go today. In fact, I was all packed. Jim and I planned to leave at daylight this morning. I went out and did a little scouting, and then decided against moving. I still may be off in a cloud [of dust] if the opportunity presents itself, as it doesn't look as if we'll leave here for at least a week or so, now. My better judgment tells me to stay but that lust for a little sight-seeing is pressing me hard, too. Satan, get behind me!

The war, which is still going on, is pretty much a forgotten subject around here. People are funny creatures! A week ago we would have been perfectly content with the conditions, but now—nix!

Roberts and Orr took off today and evidently got out, as they haven't returned. Knobly, Young, Osborn and Lordon were intercepted by a colonel and returned. Whitney was taken to the hospital today with a pretty bad case of pleurisy.

May 7

2200. And so, after all these months and years, the great struggle in Europe has come to an end! This news was taken around here as just one of those things. I was listening to the BBC with two or three other fellows at the time it was announced, and it didn't even cause us to comment. I am bewildered, not by the fact that it's over, but that hearing about it just didn't mean anything to us. The radio said New York was going mad and London was preparing to go to town tomorrow. I thoroughly expected the barracks, what's left of them, to be torn down—but nobody did a damn thing.

The war was over for us a week ago, and all we're interested in now is getting out of here. So it's officially over—what the hell!

A British paratrooper colonel announced today that we would definitely be out of here in a few days.

A Russian USO show in camp today was very good, with Russian music and a newsreel of the Yalta conference.

An officers' club is being started up—to serve beer and Jerry liquor.

May 10

Three days have slipped by. Can't have that, but I've been takin' it easy. I guess you'd call it trying to get into a little mischief—and I succeeded a little. Best not to tell about it here, as you never know whose hands these books will fall into. I'm sure to remember it though. [One possibility is that Pratt visited the nearby concentration camp, as photographs in his wartime collection include several that show piles of emaciated bodies stacked up in railcars and outside barracks.]

Usual army camp law is fast becoming laid down around here. MPs swarm everywhere and it's difficult to get off the peninsula. If you do succeed and get caught, it means a day or so in the cooler. The cooler is so full that some of the offenders are being kept in one of the barracks.

Colonel Spicer replaced Zemke yesterday. In his short speech at the opening of the officers club last night, he told us to not keep feeling sorry for ourselves, that he thought it was pretty nice around here, and that he didn't know when the hell we'd leave. He is a gruff gentleman but he speaks the truth and I think he is much better suited for the job, although Zemke has done a lot of hard work with the Russkies. Colonel Spicer was the commander of this compound until the 25th of October, when he made his memorable speech at roll call. He was charged with inciting mutiny and sentenced to be shot on March 14. He was granted an appeal and the ending of the war saved him further trial. He spent all the time in between in Solitary.

Colonel Henry Spicer, a P-51 Mustang pilot and commander of the 357th Fighter Group, was shot down and captured on March 5, 1944. As commanding officer of the 1800 men in Stalag Luft I's North II compound, he consistently antagonized his German captors while demanding that they adhere to the Geneva Convention in their treatment of POWs. His "memorable speech" began with a request that a missing steel bar be returned, or the Germans would cut off the coal ration. He then spoke of a fellow officer, Major Fred Bronson, who had been sent to the cooler for failing to obey the order of German officer ("that is beside the point") and for failing to salute a German officer of lower rank. Spicer reminded the POWs that the Geneva Convention required them only to salute German officers of equal or higher rank. He also observed that too many men appeared to be making friends with the Germans. "They are still our enemies and are doing everything they can to win the war... They are a bunch of murderous no-good liars, and if we have to stay here for 15 years to see all the Germans killed, then it will be worth it." A few of Spicer's fellow POWs, who recognized the momentous quality of the speech, wrote down as much as they could remember of it afterwards—and the steel bar re-appeared, so coal rations continued without interruption. [www.merki.com/spicerruss.htm]

Marshal Rokossovsky spoke to us yesterday and "wished for us to celebrate with him the ending of the war." He promised we would be out soon, possibly in four days. We had quite a little celebration the night before last. Flares, looted from the airfield, were shot off by the hundreds and made a really pretty show. The shutters that blacked us out at night were torn off and burned in a huge bonfire. The remaining guard towers were burned and at a minute after midnight a bust of Goebbels was thrown on the fire. Singing and accordion playing continued on into the wee hours. Thus, the war was finished here. Most all of the barbed wire has been torn down now, and it is hard to imagine that only two weeks ago we were thoroughly caged. Time works wonders. We went on a tour of the airport today. Beautiful field. The Jerries left fifteen or so planes, but they don't look so dangerous now.

People in Barth are very friendly, especially if they're close to where the Russkies happen to be standing.

I wrote home today. Weather is really nice and I'm getting a pretty good tan.

The officers' club is really swanky, thanks to a few articles looted from the Jerry officers' quarters at the flak school. A really hot five-piece band played last night, and believe it or not, fudge was served. I find this rather amusing when I think back on other clubs. We may get some liquor yet.

May 16

1000. It seems weeks since I last wrote in this gadget [the YMCA blue book that served as the third volume of Pratt's POW diaries]. That could be due to all the activity on the part of the evacuation, etc. After all the hustle and bustle mentioned above, about fifty ships [B-17s] arrived on the 12th, at about 1400 hours. Nothing ever looked so good to me, and I kind of got the feeling that this thing was over. The Krieges went mad at the first sight of the ships, and well they should have. The evacuation plans were made and carried out wonderfully well, in order of sick and wounded, British, South, and North 1, 2 and 3. We, naturally, were not out the first day and only about 900 in the first two categories were evacuated. But needless to say, it was one of those "wonderful feeling" occasions, as we were assured of being moved the next day.

That night there were big bonfire flares and general celebrations. We made fudge by the gob, as we had plenty of everything and could afford to be extravagant for once.

The ships were due to arrive at 0700 on the morning of the 13th. Kriege were up at 5 a.m., some before that. The morning dawned pretty foggy and cast a lot of gloom around, but the sun burned its way through by 7 a.m., and shortly thereafter the first group of thirty-six ships appeared.

The evacuation went off like clockwork. We were scheduled to leave for the airport between 9 and 11 a.m., and got off promptly at 10. "Fatboy" and I were on KP duty, and we dropped everything when we were alerted. I had been packed for two days, so all I had to do was grab my hat and suitcase and be off. The Russians transported our bags to the airport, so it made the three-mile hike a nice walk. The streets of Barth, which we marched through, echoed with the old familiar "Working On The Railroad" and "I Got Sixpence," for it was really an occasion. The Russkies saluted and the German people, no longer their old arrogant selves, just stood by and looked bewildered. We were on our first leg home.

In parties of thirty, we were loaded onto B-17s that didn't bother to cut their engines. At 12:42 p.m., eight months almost to the hour since I had last been in a plane, we took off—our destination, France.

The pilot flew at about 1000 feet over the Ruhr district. Such destruction is impossible to describe, it can only be seen. Towns were completely wiped out. Cologne was leveled worse than Cassino [Monte Cassino, Italy], and I thought that was bad. It was a humble yet gratifying sight to see what the Jerries asked for—and received.

Contrary to my previous thoughts, I didn't feel too uneasy at riding in the air again.

We landed outside Rheims at 17:35 p.m. Pretty French Red Cross gals brought us lemonade and donuts. From there, we moved in trucks forty-five miles south to a tent city. GI chow once more. Plenty of good fried chicken. Back into Rheims at 0800 the next morning. Boarded a hospital train for the next stop, Camp Lucky Strike. [This was one of a series of U.S. Army "tent cities" set up around the French port of Le Havre after the D-Day invasion in June, 1944, and named after popular brands of cigarettes—so the "cigarette diaries" conclude in a "cigarette camp"!]

Arrived here at 4:30 a.m. yesterday morning. Really a huge place. All tents and dirty as hell. It was formerly a big invasion camp but is now a clearing post for POWs. There must be 60,000 men here now. Things are badly screwed up in general, but I don't mind too much because I know it won't be long before I'll be homeward bound. POWs were being cleared in four days before so many were unloaded; it takes from eight to twelve days now. The best sight of all around here is hundreds of German POWs doing the dirty work.

Knobly, Braca and I saw a little of the surrounding country yesterday, and it is beautiful. We are close to Dieppe here, and the beach is about two miles away. There are plenty remnants of battles and fortifications left, so we must be careful of mines, etc. Had my first drink in months and it was good French wine. We have no money, but cigarettes are better than wine anyhow. I expect to see much more of the French country before I leave—Paris, I hope.

May 19

Still holding out at Camp Lucky Strike. I've done very little these past three days. Moved to a new area in camp, which is much better organized. The food is damn good—chicken most of the time. We don't have anything to do but eat and sleep or whatever we fancy doing that is within the realm. Knobly and I went into St. Valery last night (four miles) and had several cognacs and cider. Knobly had borrowed money (500 francs) from someone, but at 35 francs a drink that didn't last long.

Some GIs leaving for home today did all right by us, however. It felt pretty good to get a little buzzed again. I dodged MPs and went back today and got a haircut—a good one, for a change. Beautiful country around here. I expect to move to "D" area for processing any day now. Saw Bierney, now on Shelor's crew. He said Shelor had left already. I looked up some group members who have passed through. There are a lot of them, but more that I didn't know.

This is the final entry in The Cigarette Diaries. *Frank Pratt and his fellow B-24 officer crewmates from Stalag Luft I, Daniel Blodgett, Irving Canin and George Winter shipped out to the United States in June, 1945. Frank was promoted to 1st Lieutenant before being honorably discharged from military service 30 days later.*

Technical Sergeant Vernon Christensen, survived his horrendous series of "death marches" across Germany and ended up in Camp Lucky Strike at the same time as the other four men, though none of them were aware of this at the time. Christensen was ill, but he was worried that he might be left behind and concealed his illness until he was safely aboard ship. He was immediately sent to the sickbay and was still ill when his ship arrived in the U.S. He spent the next month in an Army hospital before returning to his home in Montana.

Frank Pratt returned to his home in Blanchard, Washington where, one imagines, he had a few of those "dream meals" to help himself re-adjust to non-Kriege life. He and Georgia eventually divorced. He met and married his second wife, Helene, while she was keeping the books for his service station. He sold that business in the mid-1950s and bought into a co-operatively-owned plywood mill in nearby Anacortes, Washington, from which he retired in 1979. Frank and Helene had one child, their daughter Rebecca. Helene died in 1980. In 1985, Frank married his longtime acquaintance Bernice Nicholson and moved with her back to Blanchard, where they pursued their shared love of gardening and rural life on the property where Frank had been raised by his aunt—the same property he referred to in his diaries when he was daydreaming of home.

Frank Pratt passed away on October 19, 2008.

Seven Skagit Youths Liberated from Prison Camps

(Special to The Herald)

MOUNT VERNON, May 24.—Direct word from seven Skagit county youths who have been held as prisoners of war in Germany has been received by local parents, it was revealed here Tuesday, and all are now on their way home. Messages from the Skagit boys are being received through the POW division of the American Red Cross, Mrs. Hugo Thiret, local chairman, announced.

Skagit youths who have been released and from whom word has been received include the following:

Pfc. Robert C. Byham, Sedro-Woolley; Kelsey J. Latham, Burlington; Elmer Cabe, Lyman; Lieut. Stanley Czech, Mount Vernon; Lieut. Frank Hayden, Mount Vernon; Sgt. Edwin L. Gee, Lyman; and Lieut. Frank J. Pratt, Blanchard. Several other Skagit youths are known to have been held in internment camps, but as yet no word has been received.

The Bellingham Herald, F

Expected Home

Lieut. Frank J. Pratt, of Blanchard, who was a German prisoner in Stalag Luft I since he was shot down over Poland last September, was in France waiting to board ship for home when he wrote to his wife May 19, his letter just received. He said he expected to be home by the last week in June.

Lt. F. J. Pratt

Former student at Western Washington college, and operator of a service station at Prospect and Holly streets when he entered service in February, 1943, Lieutenant Pratt was serving with the Fifteenth air force in Italy as a B-24 bombardier when he was shot down. He has the Distinguished Flying Cross, the Air Medal and two oak leaf clusters.

Choice rumors

Moving to Sweden.

Guns are removed from the Siegfried Line.

Red Cross Parcels are in.

Krieges will be pro-rated one grade in rank upon return to US.

All Krieges will be paid $2.50 extra a day for every day spent as a POW, as a "hardship payment."

Epilogue

In Wadowice, Poland, on September 13, 1944, local villagers had watched Frank Pratt's burning B-24 fall in pieces from the sky. Some of the crew members parachuted to earth; six others were trapped in the plane all the way to the ground. German soldiers who arrived at the crash site reportedly clubbed the bodies of the six dead Americans and stripped them of clothing, watches and dog-tags, before ordering the villagers to bury the remains in a common grave. The villagers were permitted to mark the grave site with a cross, and several young women brought flowers and prayed for the souls of the dead airmen, though the Germans threatened to send them to the nearby Osweicim (Auschwitz) concentration camp if they were caught doing this again. The villagers did not forget the Americans, however, and at the end of the war a larger monument was built to honor their sacrifice in the fight against Nazi oppression.

In October 1947, a unit from the U.S. Army Graves Registration Service arrived in Wadowice to investigate the crash site. The remains of the airmen were unidentifiable, but records from the Fifteenth Air Force of aircraft reported shot down or missing in that vicinity, together with POW records and information about the date of crash provided by the villagers, strongly indicated that the bodies were those of Pratt's six missing crewmen: William Lawrence, Matthew Hall, Everett MacDonald, William Eggers, Arthur Nitsche and Lewis Kaplan. Their identities were confirmed by follow-up forensic work, and in 1949 the remains were exhumed for re-interment in the U.S. or U.S. military cemeteries in Western Europe.

The story might have ended there, as ongoing commemoration by the villagers of the American bomber crew was officially discouraged during the Cold War and the monument at the gravesite was dismantled. After the Soviet Union collapsed at the end of 1991, Poland regained its political freedom and the monument was rebuilt using a portion of the fuselage of the plane. In January 1992, Donald Rice, then-Secretary of the U.S. Air Force made an official visit to Poland and was asked to lay a wreath on the monument. Village leaders in Wadowice also asked him to identify the six dead airmen. Air Force historian Daniel Mortenson was assigned to research the matter and to attempt to locate any surviving crewmen. He tracked down Pratt, Winter, Christensen and Blodgett and pieced together the events of September 13, 1944, and their aftermath. (Irving Canin was still alive at that time also, but his whereabouts was not discovered until 2003.)

Information about the crew was sent back to Poland, and the names of the six dead airmen were carved into the base of the Wadowice monument. A petition was also sent by a community leader in Wadowice to the President of Poland requesting that the survivors among the crew, together with the families of the deceased, be awarded Polish military medals. On August 30, 1994, Frank Pratt, George Winter, Vernon Christensen and Daniel Blodgett attended a reception at the Polish Embassy in Washington D.C., where they were presented with the Polish Home Army Cross. Frank was accompanied on this occasion by his wife, Bernice, daughter, Rebecca, and Rebecca's partner, Don Garrido. The sisters of co-pilot Matthew Hall, who was killed in the crash, attended the reception also, and accepted the award on behalf of their brother.

Rebecca Pratt recalls: "At the conclusion of the medals ceremony, as we all stood in a group in front of the stage, a man approached us. He apologized for interrupting and introduced himself as Stanislaw Przystal. He told us he was Polish and worked for the Polish government. He happened to be in Washington D.C. that week and had been invited to attend the evening's event. Without knowing that it would involve a ceremony, he had agreed to come because it was something social to do while he was in D.C. Then his eyes began to well up and he explained that he had been a teenager in Wadowice in September,1944, and had seen men parachute out of the burning plane before it crashed to the ground. The experience affected him deeply, and he had wondered time and again over the years what had happened to the 'soldiers' who had been captured that day. Now, as he looked from one crew member to the next, his tears began to flow. 'I can't believe my questions have just been answered,' he said. 'Thank you!'"

Frank Pratt (at left) and his surviving B-24 crewmates from the September 13, 1944, mission over Osweicim: Vernon Christensen, Daniel Blodgett and George Winter, wearing their Polish Home Army Cross medals after a ceremony at the Polish Embassy, Washington D.C., August 30, 1994.

A week after the Polish Embassy reception, Vernon Christensen traveled to Wadowice, Poland, to attend a fiftieth anniversary commemoration of the crash. The memorial site has since become a tourist attraction of sort for Americans who visit Wadowice, which is otherwise famous as the birthplace of Pope John Paul II, Karol Wojtyla.

The inscription on the Wadowice monument reads: "On this spot on 13 September, 1944 six American Airmen died in a battle for Polish freedom."

The memorial site in Wadowice, Poland.

References

Mortenson, Daniel R., Downed Aircrew Over Europe: Revival of Polish Affection at the End of the Cold War. *Air Power History*, Spring 1993, 44-51

Whiting, Jerry W., *Don't Let the Blue Star Turn Gold. Walnut Creek*, CA: Tarnaby, 2005

www.485thbg.org

www.b24.net/pow/stalag1.htm

www.merkki.com/spicerruss.htm

www.merkki.com/zemkehubert.htm

https://en.wikipedia.org/wiki/Camp_Fünfeichen

https://en.wikipedia.org/wiki/Death_of_Benito_Mussolini

https://en.wikipedia.org/wiki/Death_of_Adolf_Hitler

http://www.deathcamps.org/reinhard/himmlercap.html

Frank Pratt with his daughter Rebecca, Blanchard, Washington, 2006

.

Made in the USA
San Bernardino, CA
26 August 2016